Finding God the Father

✝✝✝

A Jubilee Retreat

By
Rev. Msgr. Richard L. Carroll

The Author

Rev. Msgr. Richard L. Carroll has been the Pastor of St. Margaret Mary Church, Slidell, Louisiana, since January 17, 1970. He is the author of *A Priest Looks at Medjugorje*, *The Remnant Church* and *The Third Millennium: The Triumph of Our Lady*. His brother, Rev. Msgr. Ralph Carroll is Pastor of St. Clement of Rome in Metairie, Louisiana. They have a sister, Yvonne Hymel who is married to Anthony Hymel. The Hymel's have five children. Father Carroll's parents are the late Ralph Carroll, Sr. and Myrlie Gremillion Carroll.

First Edition

Printed by Sheridan Books, Inc.

Manufactured in the United States of America
ISBN# 0-9643572-2-4

Library of Congress Catalog Card No: 99-093427

Copies of this book may be obtained from:
Queenship Publishing
Attn: Mr & Mrs. Bob Schaeffer
C & 4th Street, Bldg. 10
Strother Field
Winfield, Kansas 67156
FAX: (805) 957-1631
PHONE: 1-800-647-9882

Table of Contents
Finding God the Father
A Jubilee Retreat

Dedication

This book is dedicated and consecrated to God our Heavenly Father and to the Immaculate Heart of Mary, daughter of the Father, Spouse of the Holy Spirit and mother of Jesus Christ, the Son of God. May you be protected in the Heart of Mary until she presents you to the Father, as His beloved son or adorable daughter.

Acknowledgements

I would like to express my sincere gratitude to Mrs. Shannon Gallo, without whom this book would never have been produced. I would like to thank Mr. Glenn Sablich, owner of Graci Graphics, for the cover work. I am also grateful to the parishioners of St. Margaret Mary Church in Slidell, Louisiana, who willingly gave their testimonies at our parish retreat and allowed us to share them with you. I am also indebted to Fr. Henri Nouwen, author of *The Return of the Prodigal Son* and Fr. Joseph Breault, author of *Seeking Purity of Heart.* These works were clear signposts for me in my journey to the Father. I highly recommend both of these books.

Introduction

The Holy Father, Pope John Paul II, has asked the clergy to prepare their flock for the Third Millenium. The American Bishops have taken up this challenge and suggested a number of ways that priests could prepare their parishioners for the Great Jubilee. One of their suggestions was a Parish Retreat.

At St. Margaret Mary Church in Slidell, Louisiana, we decided to put on a "Life in the Spirit" retreat. For 15 years we have offered this type of retreat to our confirmation classes in the 11th and 12th grades. Seven years ago we began the same type of retreat for 8th graders. Would this work using adults, sharing their Catholic faith? This small book is our offering to you.

Letter to Parishioners - March 30, 1999

I am happy to report to you that the plans for our Parish Retreat at St. Margaret Mary are going very well. This retreat will be held in the church Friday, June 4 through Sunday, June 6. The details of the retreat are spelled out in the enclosed literature. Presently 815 parishioners 16 and older have signed up. If for any reason you cannot come, I would ask that you notify my office. You will receive free reserved tickets in the mail a week in advance.

I am planning to be in Fatima, Portugal on a pilgrimage with the Opus Sanctorum Angelorum group from May 8-20, 1999. You may wonder why I decided to go to Fatima instead of Garabandal. I was thrilled with the "possibility" that I might see the great Eucharistic Miracle predicted by Our Lady to occur in Garabandal. Mary promised that those who were present would be healed of their physical afflictions. With a paralyzed vocal cord and extremely poor eyesight, I was hoping to prolong my effectiveness as a Pastor if Our Lady cured me. But this was not her plan.

In my sermon of December 17, 1998, I explained that I would go to Garabandal on May 13, 1999 provided:

    A. The warning and the 8-day notice by Conchita occur.

    B. The Holy Father promulgates the final dogma that Mary is Co-redemptrix and Mediatrix of all graces.

Unfortunately, neither of these two conditions occurred. I received a letter from a Marian group in Australia saying, "We have reason to believe that Joey Lamangino, the Apostle of Garabandal, will be in Rome for the Beatification of Padre Pio on May 2, 1999 and go on to Garabandal for May 13." I called Joey in New York to ask if this were true. "No Father," Joey replied. "The world-wide warning has not occurred nor have we been warned by Conchita to go to Garabandal for May 13th. Therefore, I will not be there in May." That was good enough for me. I plan to be in Fatima May 13, 1999.

Why go to Fatima now?

I realize I need a healing. No, not of my paralyzed vocal cord nor even of my eyesight. I have been blind since I was 22 in my right eye. My eye doctor has been reluctant to operate on my left eye, which has a cataract, for fear that if something goes wrong, I will be permanently blind. I also wanted to see the great Eucharistic Miracle because Our Lady made a promise. "After the miracle, if people convert, the tribulation can be averted," Mary said.

I now realize that I need to be healed of the hurt I felt in 1960 when the third secret of Fatima was not made public. I did not blame the church, as I should have, but Mary herself. What kind of mother would give her children a warning and then refuse to make it public? I lived through the time of the Great Apostasy.

In 1960, as a young priest I saw 85% of Catholics attending Mass every Sunday. Today it is about 30%. One hundred thousand priests deserted their priesthood, leaving us to pick up the pieces. We were scorned and shamed, and I blamed my Mother Mary. I need to go to Fatima and ask for her forgiveness. I have loved her with an unquenchable love since my first moments of my memory. I want to tell her I am sorry.

For my lack of trust that she would care for me even if I became a blind priest, I must ask her forgiveness. In a mental hospital in 1994 and facing death from heart surgery in 1995, Our Lady clearly spoke to my heart. "As long as I am near you, what do you have to fear?" Mary said. For my lack of trust, I must go to Fatima and ask forgiveness.

The Smile that Conquers Fear

Early one morning, in prayer, I saw myself as a child of one or two years old. I had been nurtured in my mother's womb in fear. Mom had lost two or three children through miscarriage. I had been weaned too soon because she had to care for my older brother who was sickly. I so wanted to please my mother…but she would never smile at me. A smile would chase the fear out of my heart. Yet mother seldom smiled at this little baby boy.

I began to get the connection. When I look at many of you I see my own mother. You are burdened with your trials and tribulations. You find it hard to smile. That little child inside is shouting to his mother… "Mom, just smile and we will get through this together…your smile will cure my fear."

Letter to Parishioners - May 23, 1999

I was pleased to learn that you signed up for our Parish Retreat on June 4-6, 1999. As I indicated to you earlier

June 6 will be my 40th Anniversary as a priest. Nearly 900 adults and older teens have signed up for this Parish Retreat. The closing Mass will be the culmination of a life of joy which I have had in serving God our Father as a priest of Jesus Christ. Nearly 30 of these years have been at St. Margaret Mary. I thank God our Father for each one of you my children. Your presence at the closing Mass will truly be the highlight of my life. For your years of faithful service to the Church and this Parish, I thank you from the bottom of my heart.

Our Holy Father has asked Pastors to prepare for the Great Jubilee 2000. The American Bishops have suggested that one of the best ways to prepare for the coming celebration is by holding Parish Missions. Your presence is simply another sign of your willingness to do whatever is asked to help prepare us to become a Remnant Church. Loyalty to the Holy Father, like love of Our Lady and respect for the Eucharist are hallmarks of this parish. We are now preparing for the year of the Lord's favor…the Jubilee 2000.

In his first sermon at Nazareth, Jesus was asked to preach. He was handed the scroll from the Prophet Isaiah. Jesus read this: "The Spirit of the Lord is on me; therefore he has anointed me. He has sent me to bring glad tidings to the poor, to proclaim liberty to captives, recovery of sight to the blind and release to prisoners. To announce a year of favor from the Lord."(Luke 4:18-19) Then Jesus, like Rabbis of his time, sat down to preach. He began by saying, "Today this scripture passage is fulfilled in your hearing."(Luke 4:21)

Now 2000 years after the birth of Jesus, our Holy Father, Pope John Paul II, is proclaiming a "Year of the Lord's Favor". The Pope has asked us in 1999 to focus on God the Father. Our retreat is entitled "Finding God the Father".

Father John Powell, S.J.

"Will I ever find God?" the young student at Loyola Chicago asked his religion teacher as he dropped off his final exam. Fr. Powell knew that Tom fancied himself an atheist. He didn't believe in God. What was the priest going to reply?

"No Tom, I don't think you will ever find God", the young Jesuit replied. "But Tom, one day God will find you", the priest said.

Ten years later Tom came to visit Fr. Powell in his office. He had heard that Tom was dying of cancer. "Tom, how does it feel to be 30 years old and dying?" the priest asked. Tom replied, "Oh it could be worse Father, I could be 50 years old and think that life is only about booze, broads and making money. Something interesting happened to me. When I first learned I had terminal cancer I began to pray for the first time in years...If there is a God up there, help me," Tom pleaded, but nothing happened.

"Then I remembered something you told us," Tom continued. "You said, 'Wouldn't it be a terrible thing to go through life and never tell those we love how we feel?' So one day I sat my Dad down and said to him, 'Dad I have been nothing but a pain in the ass my entire life. I have caused you nothing but trouble. But now that I know I am dying, I want to say one thing to you. Dad, I love you.' For the first time in my memory, my father began to cry. He wrapped his arms around my neck and sobbed uncontrollably. 'Tom, I love you too,' my dad said. We spent the entire night talking and something happened that night as we shared our love. God found me," Tom concluded.

It is my hope that during our Parish Retreat, God our Merciful Father will welcome home some of His sons and

9

daughters who have left the church...who have abandoned Jesus Christ...that God will find you! Amazingly, the return to the Father of the Prodigal son is far easier than the return of the Older Brother to the heart of God the Father. He represents the nominal Catholics. These individuals resent the gift of their baptism. Frequently they "never did anything seriously wrong". And yet Jesus gave them a warning: "I know your deeds; I know you are neither hot nor cold. ... But because you are lukewarm, neither hot nor cold, I will spew you out of my mouth!"(Revelation 3:15-16.)

God Our Merciful Father

We now have a replica of a famous painting by Rembrandt. It is entitled *God - Our Merciful Father*. I have taken the statue of the Sacred Heart and placed it in the vestibule. For the rest of 1999, we will keep the picture of God our Father on the left side of the altar. That side altar is dedicated as an Altar of Intercession.

The theme of Rembrandt's painting represents the spiritual homecoming of all humankind. It shows the prodigal son being welcomed back by his father. To one side, the elder brother looks on and in the background are other unknown figures who like ourselves contemplate the scene.

Rembrandt, a Dutch artist, painted the original picture in 1669. The artist pursued the mystery of light. In this picture he mingles light and darkness in a way that suggests a rising dawn, a burst of sunlight or more deeply the mystery of a resurrection. The central figures of the father and son form a glowing focus. With a gentle, bending gesture of love, the Father welcomes back his son. This is a God who always takes the first initiative, who stoops to us, gently beckoning and holding us close. We need only have the insight to recognize the home to which we truly belong. Julian of Norwich has a wonderful phrase in her

Showings in which she describes God as "The Astonishing Familiarity of Home", a phrase very close to Jesus' own words, when he says, "Live on in me, as I do in you." (John 15:4)

Understanding the Process of the Retreat

Our Parish Retreat will be our opportunity to find God the Father. The focus on Friday night is the recognition that we are sinners and that it is Jesus who saves us. Friday night will culminate with a Healing of Ancestry Mass and Deliverance prayer. Just as there was an acute rivalry between the prodigal son and the older son, so too in our own families we need the healing touch of God upon our entire ancestry.

I am enclosing a Genogram with this letter as well as an explanation by Fr. Al Fredette, M.S. All of us inherit good and bad genes from our ancestors. It is important that we be healed of all negative influences from the past up to the third and fourth generation and all generations before these where healing has not occurred.

In the book of Exodus 20:5-6, we read "For I, the Lord, your God, am a jealous God, inflicting punishment for their fathers' wickedness on the children of those who hate me, down to the third and fourth generation; but bestowing mercy down to the thousandth generation, on the children of those who love me and keep my commandments." The healing of ancestry is sometimes referred to as Intergenerational Healing of the family tree. The Genogram is the family history for you and your spouse. Fill out as much as you can. Bring in your Genogram on Friday night where we will have the Mass of inner healing. We may not know many of the members of our family. Bring your record even if you have only the names of you, your spouse and your children. Friday night is a time to heal the family tree. We will place all of the Genograms on the altar of intercession under the picture of God our Merciful Father.

Saturday the conversion experience continues with an emphasis on the Eucharist and Our Blessed Mother. Sunday night will culminate with Divine Mercy-The Last Hope of Salvation. Having experienced our own conversion, we turn our eyes to God the Father and ask to be a community of intercessors. You are going to experience perhaps for the first time the love of God our Father. The Sunday night Mass will be my 40th anniversary as a priest. I want the opportunity of introducing you as my children to God the Father.

Rembrandt's Prodigal Son

The gift that I wish for each of you parishioners of St. Margaret Mary can be summed up in one phrase. I pray that you never forget that you are the beloved sons; you are precious daughters of God the Father.

During the week, we had a copy of Rembrandt's famous painting mounted over our Altar of Intercession to my right. The original Rembrandt was purchased by Catherine the Great who acquired it for Russia. It has been kept in St. Petersburg. The original painting is 8' x 6'. It was the last painting done by this Dutch artist, Rembrandt who died at the age of 63. The painting is entitled, *The Return of the Prodigal Son* and it involves the mystery of **returning home** to the Father.

Characters in Painting

You notice that God the Father is holding the prodigal son. There are four bystanders. The tall young man is the older son in the parable account of Jesus (script. Ref. Luke 15:11-32). There are two women and two men as bystanders.

I am indebted to Fr. Henri Nouwen who wrote a book entitled *The Return of the Prodigal Son: A Story of Homecoming.* The book is a journey that I want you to take with me to an inner place. You will hear God the Father say to you, "You are my beloved son...you are my precious daughter." Fr. Nouwen's book is a prophetic vision looking at life through God the Father's eyes. This French priest went from teaching at Harvard University to living as he does today with a community that works with retarded children. Come with me on this journey. You are called to enter the inner sanctuary of your being where God has chosen to dwell.

The First Phase – Being the Younger Son

The long years of university teaching had left Fr. Nouwen feeling quite lost. At the end of it all, he felt homeless and very tired. The second phase in his spiritual journey was initiated while talking about Rembrandt's painting to Bart Gavigan, a friend from England. "I wonder if you are not more like the elder son?" Bart asked.[i]

Fr. Nouwen began to think of himself as the elder son. Nouwen is the oldest child in the family. He lived a dutiful life. When he was six Nouwen decided to become a priest and never changed his mind. "I was born, baptized, confirmed and ordained in the same church and had always been obedient to my parents, my teachers, my bishops and my God. I had never run away from home, never wasted my time and money on sensual pursuits, and had never gotten lost in debauchery." The priest concluded, "For my entire life I had been quite responsible, traditional and homebound. But, with all of that, I may, in fact have been just as lost as the younger son. ... I saw my jealousy, my anger, my touchiness ... and sullenness, and, most of all, my subtle self-righteousness. ... my thinking and feeling was ridden with resentment. ... I was the elder son for sure, but just as lost as his younger brother, even though I had stayed 'home' all my life."[ii]

After celebrating thirty years as a priest, Fr. Nouwen experienced inner anguish. He could no longer feel safe in his own community and began to work on his inner healing. He found great consolation in reading about the tormented life of the great Dutch painter Rembrandt and his agonizing journey that ultimately led him to paint his magnificent work. In his Hermitage at Daybreak Community, a group that cares for retarded children, Fr. Nouwen began the third phase of his spiritual journey.

One of his friends said to Nouwen." You have been looking of friends all your life' you have be craving for affection as long as I've known you; ... you have been begging for attention, appreciation and affirmation left and right. The time has come to claim your true vocation - to be a father who can welcome his children home without asking them any questions and without wanting anything from them in return. ... We, at Daybreak, ... need you to be a father who can claim for himself the authority of true compassion."[iii]

The Younger Son Leaves

The full title of Rembrandt's painting is *The Return of the Prodigal Son.* The young son's leaving is tantamount to wishing his father dead. Since I won't be around until you die, the young son asks for his entire inheritance. With reluctance, the father gives it to him. It is a heartless rejection not only of his father but the very home he grew up in. It is a betrayal of the treasured values of family and community.

The parable of the prodigal son expresses the boundless love and mercy of God the Father. It is all about God the Father's great mercy to us, his children. In Rembrandt's painting the father touches the son, the son is leaning against the father's breast. The story deals not with the human love of an earthly father. What is meant and represented is the Divine Love and Mercy in its power to transform death into life.

Searching for Love Where it Can Not be Found

The world tells you that the keys to self-fulfillment lie in the accumulation of wealth, power, attainment of status, lavish consumption of food and drink, and sexual gratification without distinguishing between lust and love. As long as we live within the world delusions, our addictions condemn us to futile quests in a distant country. "The addicted life can ... be designated a life lived in 'a distant country.'"[iv]

Fr. Nouwen writes, "I am the prodigal son every time I search for unconditional love where it cannot be found. ... Why do I keep leaving home where I am called a child of God, the Beloved of my Father? ... It's almost as if I want to prove to myself ... that I do not need God's love, ... I want to be fully independent. Beneath it all is the great rebellion ... the unspoken curse: "I wish you were dead."[v]

The Elder Son

As you view Rembrandt's painting you realize the hardest conversion is that of the one who stayed home. You notice in the painting that the elder son is unwilling to participate in the Father's welcome. Will he come closer and embrace his younger brother or will he walk away in anger and disgust? Rembrandt's painting could have been called the parable of the lost sons.

Lost in Resentment

The older brother did not have the courage to run away but he was lost in resentment. Obedience and duty became a burden and service became slavery. Outwardly, the older son did all the right things. People respected him, but when confronted by his father's joy at the return of his younger brother, a dark power erupts in him and boils to the surface. You see he is resentful, proud, unkind and selfish, one that had faults hidden deeply within.

The older son was angry with his father and refused to go to the celebration...joy and resentment cannot coexist. I do not know whether the elder son was reconciled with his younger brother, what I do know is the Heart of the Father is made up of limitless mercy.

Father Nouwen writes, "It is clear that alone, ... I cannot find myself. ... There is no doubt ... because I have tried so hard in the past to heal myself from my complaints and failed...and failed...and failed, until I came to the edge of complete emotional collapse and physical exhaustion. I can only be healed from above, where God reaches down. What is impossible for me is possible for God. 'With God, everything is possible.'"[vi]

God the Father's Love

While I was in Fatima Our Lady woke me at 4:00 a.m. on May 13, the Anniversary of the Fatima apparitions. I had asked God the Father for three things, the cure of my eyes (I am blind in one eye and have cataracts on both eyes), the cure of my voice, and the Heart of God the Father. Our Lady spoke to my heart; "I can get you only one of these three, which do you wish?" I asked for the Heart of God the Father. Mary seemed pleased.

When I visited the church where the three visionaries were baptized in Fatima, Portugal, I was told of a 15th century statue in the rear of the church. When I went to the back, I found to my amazement, a copy of the painting of Rembrandt's Prodigal Son. I knew immediately that understanding the Heart of God the Father will unlock keys to our spiritual survival. For at one time or other each of us will be the prodigal child or the older son or daughter.

16

God the Father is seen, in Rembrandt's painting as a half-blind old man. I can now see Father, your infinite compassion, unconditional love and everlasting forgiveness. In the painting, the old blind father reaches out to all humanity. The old man seems to have cried an ocean of tears as he got caught up in our anguish and agony. I know the heart of that Father burns with an immense desire to bring his children home. Father, I beg you to use this parish retreat to bring some of your children home.

Father, I know it is not your desire to punish your children. They have punished themselves by their own inner and outward struggle. Father it is your desire to let your children know that the love they searched for in such distorted ways has been, is and always will be there for them. It is only in you Father, that we can find **UNCONDITIONAL LOVE**. Give us that unconditional love, Father.

So often Father, we have asked ourselves how am I to find God? The question would better be put, "How am I to allow God the Father, to find me? It is we who are doing the hiding.

Conclusion

In conclusion my dear children, I will share the pain of a father whose heart is deeply wounded by the suicide of one of his precious daughters in order to make an important point. No matter what happens to you in life, always remember that **ONLY GOD THE FATHER CAN GIVE YOU UNCONDITIONAL LOVE**. If you open your ears and your hearts you will hear him say, "You are my beloved son...you are my precious adorable daughter."

Chapter 1
Angels

Jesus said: "I assure you, unless you change and become like little children, you will not enter the kingdom of God."(Matthew 18:3)

"See that you never despise one of these little ones. I assure you, their angels in heaven constantly behold my heavenly father's face."(Matthew 18:10)

"'This is eternal life, that they know you the only true God, and Jesus Christ whom you sent' (John 17:3). The whole of Christian life is like a great pilgrimage to the house of the father, whose unconditional love for every human creature, and in particular for the 'prodigal son' (cf. Luke 15:11-32), we discover anew each day. This pilgrimage takes place in the heart of each person, extends to the believing community and then reaches to the whole of humanity."[vii]
(Pope John Paul, II * Tertio Millennio Adventiente)

Authors Note: On Friday night June 4,1999, our parish retreat began at St. Margaret Mary, Slidell, Louisiana. Over 600 parishioners, including adults, members of the retreat team and friends gathered in the church.

The retreat team, a group of high school and college age students opened with a skit entitled: "I wish I were a Retreatant". The cast included a nun, a stewardess, a plumber, an electrician, a preacher, an aerobics instructor, a farmer and a nurse. They got everyone in the mood of the retreat - to become like little children. Jesus told us: "I assure you, unless you change and become like little children, you will not enter the kingdom of God."(Matthew 18:3)

Alan Fries gave the first talk. Alan, who served two tours of duty in Vietnam as a helicopter pilot, spoke about being like a little child. For seven years Alan has seen angels in St. Margaret Mary Church. Frequently, when Alan is asked to speak to a group of people, he encounters others who have seen angels. There is a natural reluctance to tell others for fear they would think you "crazy'.

It takes a truly childlike person willing to risk sharing this great blessing with others. It has been may own experience through the books I have written, that as I have shared how Jesus has worked in this parish; others open their hearts and tell the great things Jesus has done in their live.

****

Alan Fries
To Be Like a Little Child

I would like to begin tonight by talking about one of my favorite subjects, Angels. Then I'd like to take a few minutes and say a few words about myself. I want to speak about myself because I'm often asked why do I see Angels? My answer is. First, I am expected to share it with you. Maybe, just maybe, you and I might feel Jesus inside us after going to communion and maybe, just maybe, we might find the hope, the courage to change. Maybe, just maybe, we might find the joy, the happiness, and the awe angels have for our Lord. The other reason. I don't know, because I see myself as the last person who should see Angels, especially with my background. There is however something about me that is different. Today, I trust God more than I ever have. I see Him as part of every moment of my life. I haven't always been this way, as you'll see. One of the things I say to folks when I go around talking about Angels is; "YOU ARE WHO YOU BELONG TO"! I ask you; do you know whom you belong to?

What follows are notes I wrote down after my first two encounters with what have become some truly wonderful friends. On July 12, 1992, as the 7:00 pm Mass began, I started to see images around the altar. As the Mass progressed, these images began to take shape. However, I already knew what they were, they were angels. I can't explain how I knew, I just did. Not only could I see them, I could feel some of their feelings. There were angels all around the altar, coming and going through the ceiling. When I started looking around, I could see angels standing next to and above a lot of the people in church. As Fr. Ken Harney consecrated the Eucharist and wine, there were several angels all around him. Some of the angels had wings, but the majority did not (or they were not visible). They were all dressed in a white garment that went almost to the floor. I could not make out their faces and they seemed to have sandy blond hair. Each of them glowed with a white light. It was a soft, warm sensation.

The next week, July 19th, things were different. Fr. Carroll celebrated the 7:00 PM Mass. I had forgotten about what had happened the previous Sunday. Then just a short time after Mass began I started to see images again. I knew and remembered at the same time, they were back. This time, there were not as many on the altar, but when Fr. Carroll stood at the altar, I now noticed in addition to the two on either side of him, a very tall angel. I could not look at this angel. When I looked around, I could look at the other angels. However, no matter how hard I tried, I could look at the body of this one, but not his face. My first thoughts were ones of "he's too terrible to look at". The first word that came to me was "horrific". Now I became confused. How could something evil be at Mass? Inside, I was torn between being drawn to look at him, or rather compelled. Yet I said to myself, "I cannot, it scares me!" There was not a sensation of fear, like being afraid of something and yet fear is the only word I can describe.

Then something really different happened. As Fr. Carroll started reading the Gospel, I saw two baby angels at the foot of the podium. They stayed for the rest of the

Mass. There were four other angels around Fr. Carroll; two on both side and right behind him was the tall angel, and I still could not look in his face. This angel followed Fr. Carroll everywhere.

Several times, I was drawn to the baby angels and they made me laugh, as did several other angels. It seemed as though they were having such a joyous time it made me giggle uncontrollably. My wife, Rosemary asked me, "What are you laughing at?" I could only respond with, "If you could only see what I see!" Then came the Hosanna. There were angels all around the altar. Some were coming and going through the ceiling, and still the tall angel stood behind Fr. Carroll. Then there appeared on either side of the altar, two more tall angels. I then asked myself, "why?" and suddenly knew. They had come to "guard" our priest and the Eucharist. I then looked around and noticed angels everywhere. When I looked back at the altar, this time I could finally look at the face of the tall angel behind Fr. Carroll. It was not frightening or evil, but one of incredible power! The closest word I can find would be "overwhelming awe", which Webster's describes as: "a mixed feeling of reverence, fear and wonder caused by something majestic, sublime, or, the power of inspiring fearful reverence." I immediately knew that these three angels on the altar were "special."

They were special protection for Fr. Carroll and the Eucharist, the Body and Blood of Christ! As I looked at the angel behind Fr. Carroll, it was as if he spoke to me. I do not remember any words, for all I could do was cry, wring my hands, and respond with a nodding of my head and continued saying, "Yes! Yes! Again and again. This happened throughout communion. I would go from laughing to crying and each time I looked at the angel, I nodded and said, "Yes". I glanced around the church and saw many, many angels. Then I began to see angels walking up the aisles with the parishioners going for communion. At times, it was almost too much to bear, for all I could do was lower my head and sob, for they, the angels, were very, very happy.

After communion, I realized that the two tall angels who had appeared earlier to each side were gone. It was as if they were no longer needed. However, the one that I first noticed with Fr. Carroll was still behind him and stayed there even as he left the Altar. As Mass ended, the angels seem to fade from view.

My Life Story

Now, let me tell you my story. I was born in Chicago. My religious background was Baptist. When we were little we went to church, the kids that is. But, it wasn't often. All I remember was the milk and donuts during Sunday School. Later, when I was 10 or 11 we moved out of Chicago to a place called Salk Village. It was the beginning of the urban sprawl. Each Sunday a bus would come through the neighborhood and we were put on the first one. One week we'd go to a Baptist Church, another week it could be a Pentecostal.

A couple of years later we moved to Chicago Heights and there I met the friends I grew up with, who were Catholic. In order to play with my friends on Sunday I had to attend church with them. So, I went to Mass. Two things I remember from that time. The kids either didn't know, or understand what was happening at Mass. In those days Mass was in Latin and hardly anyone knew what was being said. But they did know the second thing. I could not take the something everyone else was taking, the Eucharist. I didn't know it was the Eucharist, because I could not see it. People would go up, kneel and receive from the Priest. I'd ask what it was and I was told I could not receive it because I was not Catholic. I went to Mass every Sunday with my friends until one Sunday the priest talked about giving more money. I was incensed. Here I was in this church with all its gold, ivory and crystal and the gall of this man asking for more money. Our family was not well to do and we could use so much more and then hearing this. I got up and walked out. It was many years before I entered another church.

At the age of 19, I joined the Army. I was worried I'd miss the war and I wanted to get away from my family. After basic training I attended aircraft mechanic school and then Infantry Officers Candidate school (OCS). While attending OCS, I met my future bride, Rosemary. On October 6, 1967, we were married in the Catholic Church, mostly because of Rosemary's insistence. Rosemary was born and raised Catholic and she insisted that we be married that way. For me, I didn't care one way or another.

Three months later the Army sent me to Helicopter Flight School. Following this I went to Vietnam. While in Vietnam I became convinced that God was something for weak-minded people, and became an agnostic. After my second tour I was practically an atheist and was convinced, if anything, Jesus was an astronaut from another world. During each of my tours in Vietnam I left Rosemary pregnant and she had both our sons while I was gone. She wanted to baptize them and I refused. She even got me to go to church a couple of times over the years. Each time I went, I came away more convinced of my position on religion. I'd see people I worked with and knew their attitudes and ways and asked myself, how could these people come here and hear what was being said and then act the way they did at work. I got madder and more cynical.

In 1979 I was stationed with the Louisiana National Guard. Shortly after moving into our home Rosemary had several ladies from the St. Margaret Mary welcome committee drop by and invite us to come to church. There was no such committee. Rosemary insisted that we attend church and have the kids baptized. I said no way, but finally relented and I must admit that to this day I don't know why.

Father Maughn was the associate pastor at St. Margaret Mary then and he met with us. He said he would not baptize the boys until I attended the RCIA program. If I didn't come into the church he would still baptize the boys. I thought at the time; "boy is this going to be an opportunity to set this guy straight!" It wasn't anything like RCIA today, yet it changed my life. One evening, during the break, a lady approached Fr. Maughn and challenged him as to why was he giving communion to those people who didn't deserve it. I was a little distance away and pretending not to hear. She continued, you know whom I'm talking about, why do you give them communion if you believe it to be Jesus. What he said changed my life, because it was one of the reasons I too was upset and angry with God. Why did he let all this bad stuff happen? Fr. Maughn said, "Church is for imperfect people, not perfect ones. The perfect people don't need to come to church. Maybe, just maybe, by receiving Jesus into them, they might change." I had much to think about and consider. In 1981, I became Catholic. Soon after, our boys were baptized.

Throughout my military career, I have been taught to be skeptical. I had come to believe everything has a logical explanation. All you have to do is study it long enough and most of all be objective, and the truth will come out. Such is not always the case as I was beginning to find out. My life began to change that year and every year since. There is a lot more to the universe than what you can see, touch, feel, or taste.

In 1983, Rosemary and I attended a Marriage Encounter Weekend. It was on that weekend that I cried for the first time since I was twelve. I found out that Rosemary really loved me. I do not recall ever feeling loved, or even wanted. On that weekend I found out that

God loved me and it was through Rosemary that I began this most difficult of journeys, of surrendering my control of my life to the God who always wanted me to feel His Love. In doing this I started to become more open to Rosemary and other people in my life. I started to let Rosemary in, a little at first. I actually risked telling her how I felt inside. I have to admit I was scared, but Rosemary was there, she didn't laugh or make fun of me as my family had when I was a kid. Over time I found the courage to begin to let God in. This was as hard as talking to Rosemary. For so long I had lived in what I thought was the world's view of reality. A world where being strong, independent, successful, was how you were measured. I remember hearing, then saying and believing you can't be a Christian and be successful. The world is filled with a non-Christian work ethic and if you act like, or are a Christian, you'll never make it. My view of reality was being jolted.

In 1989, after 23 years in the Army, I retired. I knew that God didn't want me to fly anymore. I knew He wanted me to go into computers. I did 16 job interviews and no job. I was taking Excedrin's like they were candies; I had such bad headaches. I thought of suicide at least once a day. What was going on? I got more and more depressed. Finally I went and prayed at the foot of the statue of the Blessed Mother. I got up and as I was walking out I turned and said; are you really there, do you really care? I turned and walked out of this church. My life was a disaster. The next day the phone rang. It was a friend. He told me that Air Logistics, a helicopter company, was hiring pilots, maybe I should call. I hung up and was madder than I'd ever been. I wasn't supposed to fly anymore. I was desperate and lost. I called and got an application. A week later I was hired. My life changed again. I had just known this was not to be and yet here I was driving to New Iberia, Louisiana. All the way there I fought with my anger, my frustration. This wasn't supposed to be happening. I came to a decision that early morning. I'd gotten there early and was sitting in the parking lot waiting for the office to open.

I let go. Somehow, I found the strength to trust that somehow, someway, God was going to make this work. When we got into the helicopter to fly several days later, I felt a wave of calmness come over me, I knew this is where I'm suppose to be. God had made it work.

Since then I've had a number of different flying jobs and currently I fly sick babies and children. There is something different about me. I'm becoming very much aware that God is the God of every moment and as such, nothing happens unless He allows it. If this is so then I have a choice to make for each moment. I can do good, or I can do bad. I must choose. First, though, I must listen. And that's the theme that runs throughout my life. When I listen and then act, things work out much differently. I heard this once, from Mother Angelica. Pray as if everything depends on God. Do as if everything depends on you. So, I do. I pray a lot, listen a lot and act. I'm learning to trust God. Seldom do I get a hundred, but I'm no longer deterred. It started slowly, long ago, at least it seems that way. I'm beginning, more and more, to trust God, be open to His will in my life and most of all accept the struggles that I encounter everyday of my life. I must choose the path I will follow. I can no longer blame others. I'm learning that I must decide whom I belong to, because we all belong to someone, or something. I have learned that you are whom you belong to. I know to whom I belong.

So, I am becoming like a little child. I'm learning to trust God, to listen for Him to speak and to try and do what He wants in my life. Being like a little child doesn't mean acting foolish, or childish. It means opening myself up and letting God in, first in my heart, then into my head. I'm learning to pray more and to listen more.

Guardian Angels

Alan Fries shared his story with you about angels. I loved the fact that he has been gifted with the ability to see these angels in our church, particularly during Mass. As a pastor it is a great consolation to me to know that these heavenly beings surround us during the liturgy.

One of the most interesting things that Alan learned was that the "imaginary friends" that most of us had as small children were actually our Guardian Angels. I remember distinctively as a child that I named my angel Champion. Whenever my brother Ralph, who was a year older, wanted to go and play with someone else, I was never disturbed. "I will just play with my friend," I would tell him. I don't remember feeling lonely as a child since I always had Champion around. He kept me company.

A young woman recently told me about her young daughter and this child's experience with her Guardian Angel. The following is her short story. You may want to ask your own small children if they have an imaginary friend and what name they have given to their Guardian Angel.

A Child's Guardian Angel

Before my baby was even born, I began saying the Guardian Angel Prayer for her almost every day. I often asked my Guardian Angel to watch over her and keep her safe during those many months of pregnancy. After she was born I continued to say the Guardian Angel Prayer for her, but instead of asking my Guardian Angel to watch over her I asked her Guardian Angel to keep her safe and healthy. I also keep a Guardian Angel medal over her bed.

All new mothers know about those nights of very little sleep. For me, after a night like that when she would start to stir in the morning I would quickly start to pray, "Please Lord, just 30 more minutes. Please send her Guardian Angel and mine to sooth her back to sleep. Please Blessed Mother and Saint Anne, you were both mothers and you know how it is, just 30 more minutes. Please intercede for me. If it is your will Lord, please." Some mornings it worked and some mornings it didn't. On one particular morning, my husband was having a bad night so he ended up sleeping in the guest bedroom. I heard her start to wake up and I said my prayer. I was very tired this morning and I was having a hard time waking up. I then, very clearly, heard a man's voice softly whispering to the baby. Soothing her back to sleep. I thought, thank goodness my husband got up with her and went back to sleep. One hour later she woke up for good. After we had all been awake for some time I thanked my husband for getting up with her and asked him how he had gotten her to go back to sleep. He looked at me confused and said he had never gotten up. It was then I knew that the voice I heard was her Guardian Angel.

Babies are always looking, giggling and talking at nothing, or so adults always think. My daughter is no different, but I always thought it would be nice if that nothing was her Guardian Angel. My daughter is 18 months now and just starting to talk. She says a lot of words, but very few that anyone but her dad and I can understand. One day I was changing her diaper and she was once again saying hi and waving to what appeared to be nothing above her. I always make conversation with her so I asked "Who are you saying hi to, your Guardian Angel?" She said "yeah!" Playing along with the game I said to her "Oh really and what is your Guardian Angel's name?" Very clearly she said "Mike." We know a few Mikes but none well enough that the name would be said often enough in her presence for her to know it. So her saying Mike at all surprised me, but the fact that she said it so clearly was what got me thinking. Maybe that really is her Guardian Angel's name. So before going to bed that night I asked my Guardian Angel for three flowers of confirmation. The next morning, without thinking about my request, I dressed her in an outfit that was nothing but flowers. Later that morning I had to redress her and again I choose something with all flowers. At lunchtime I was reading something that said "If you want to send flowers..." and it clicked. While I was waiting for actual flowers I had been getting my confirmation all along. So now every night instead of just saying the Guardian Angel prayer I ask Mike, by name, to keep her safe and healthy the whole night through.

Chapter 2
Suffering

" Thus St Paul must learn from the Lord that 'my grace is sufficient for you, for my power is made perfect in weakness,' and that the sufferings to be endured can mean that 'in my flesh I complete what is lacking in Christ's afflictions for the sake of his Body, that is the Church'"
(2 Corinthians 12:9, Colossians 1:24)[viii]
(Catechism of the Catholic Church)

Author's Note: Linda Jefferson is truly a "victim soul". God the Father has called her to a time of intense suffering. Linda is a courageous woman. She shared her testimony at all of our Masses a few years ago. She established the support group S.A.V.E. (Suffering Abortion Victims Embraced), which has been instrumental in healing many individuals.

Linda was unable to deliver her talk the night of the retreat because of her intense suffering. She gave me permission to share her testimony.

In a born again experience such as this "life in the spirit retreat", it is important to understand that each of us is a sinner. A conversion experience is not possible unless we see ourselves as sinners. Later, as we explore in depth the picture of Rembrandt, it is obvious that the older brother in the parable of the Prodigal Son never experienced himself as a sinner. Hence we see how distant he is from God the Father.

The late bishop Sheen wrote: "I thank God I am a sinner, now I can have Jesus as my savior."

"Although she is holy because of her incorporation into Christ, the Church does not tire of doing penance: before

God and man *she always acknowledges as her own her sinful sons and daughters.* As *Lumen Gentium* affirms: 'The Church, embracing sinners to her bosom, is at the same time holy and always in need of being purified and incessantly pursues the path of penance and renewal.'"[ix]

Testimony of Linda Jefferson
A Story of God's love and Mercy

In my senior year of high school, still a virgin, and still preparing for the convent, I decided to tell my parents on my eighteenth birthday. But the course of my life was going to be altered and changed forever. My parents separated and began divorce proceedings. I was so angry with God that I decided to turn my back on Him and the religious life and embrace the world and everything it had to offer.

In 1971, I graduated from high school. I fell in love with a 24-year-old man. Doug and I would talk about marriage and children. When I became pregnant, I was ecstatic, but Doug was not. We ended up going to an abortion clinic in New York City to have the abortion. I allowed Doug to convince me that it was not possible to have our baby. Even though I wanted our child so desperately, I did not have the courage and strength to continue the pregnancy because I believed our relationship would end.

I, like many women, was told that my eight-week old baby was just a blob of tissue and a piece of nothing. Being taken in by the deception, the abortion took place. It was so painful I begged the abortionist to stop and four nurses held me down. The abortionist said it was too late. Our relationship ended and I moved to Florida to change my life, so I thought. I became addicted to drugs and alcohol and led a very promiscuous lifestyle.

Once again, I found myself with an unplanned pregnancy because of a one-night stand. My girlfriend convinced me because of my addiction, it would be better to have another abortion. It is sad to say but it was easier the second time because I convinced myself that I was not doing anything wrong and, of course, the clinic confirmed it. After the abortion, I stayed at my girlfriend's home and that night I came down with a fever, infection set in, and I began to hemorrhage. She rushed me to a doctor who proceeded to tell me that the abortionist, in his hurry had tore my womb, and I needed a hysterectomy.

Three doctors later, all confirming the inevitable, the hysterectomy took place. I was devastated at the news that I would never conceive another child. My happy life before the abortions turned into a nightmare after which I attempted suicide twice. It was then that I surrendered my life to God because I knew I could not continue living the way I was.

My prayer to God was to send me someone who would love me for who I was. He answered that prayer by sending me my husband Jim (of seventeen years). Still I could not find peace, happiness, and forgiveness of myself until I went to a parish priest for counseling. I felt I was losing my mind. The parish priest I went to was Father Michael McDonagh (of EWTN fame). What a blessing!

Father Michael counseled with me extensively, bringing me back to the loving arms of Jesus. Prior to a healing Mass, Fr. McDonagh shared with me about a priest friend of his who was also counseling a young lady who had an abortion. His priest friend decided to have a Mass said for the young woman's unborn child.

During the homily the young woman witnessed the Blessed Mother carrying her unborn child down the center isle of the Church. The Blessed Mother went to the altar where Jesus was standing there. They dressed the baby in white. Then when the priest told the woman her baby was in heaven, the young woman witnessed the three of them being raised up to heaven. Fr. McDonagh told me not to look for anything. Just experience the healing power of God.

I did not tell my husband about the story Fr. McDonagh shared with me. The Mass for my children, Gabriel and Cecilia were beautiful. During the homily I was crying hysterically, yet looking around to see if I could see the Blessed Mother and my children. Jim nudged me and had this angelic smile on his face, which really upset me. I knew something miraculous was taking place when Fr. McDonagh said, "Linda, know that God truly loves you and has forgiven you, and know Gabriel and Cecilia are in heaven." All of a sudden, I screamed out and an enormous peace entered the top of my head and ran down my body to the tips of my toes. I knew I had been forgiven, healed, and made whole.

After the Mass my husband turned to me and said, "Did you see her?" "No", I replied. He then told me during the homily the Blessed Mother was standing behind Fr. McDonagh holding Gabriel and Cecilia in each arm and they were smiling at me. The Blessed Mother dressed my babies in white and then when Fr. McDonagh said they were in heaven, Jim saw the three of them rise. It was then that I screamed out with so much joy in my heart. I then understood the true power of God's unconditional love and mercy.

But my story does not end there. Nine years later God revealed that I have a third child in heaven, Sarah, whom I had miscarried before the hysterectomy. I awoke one morning in excruciating pain and began to hemorrhage. I was rushed to the hospital where I was asked if I was pregnant. I responded, "No, I don't believe so." The doctor thoroughly examined me finding nothing that would determine a miscarriage and so I buried the entire experience for twelve years.

St. Margaret Mary held a mission with Father John Izral, a Spirit filled priest, who focused on the healing power of God and the gifts of the Holy Spirit. A month prior to the mission, I kept hearing a voice say to me "Sarah's praying for you and you have been chosen to represent the unborn." I thought I was loosing my mind.

The day before the mission I went into the Adoration Chapel, knelt down and began to ask God who Sarah was. I heard a loud voice say "Sarah is your daughter." I gasped and asked, "How could this be?" No sooner did I get the question out of my mouth than I had a vision of the morning of 1980 when I woke up in excruciating pain and hemorrhaging. The voice then told me I had a miscarriage and the baby's name is Sarah. I was horrified and filled with anger towards God. "Why would you let this happen?" I remember screaming to God. "Have I not suffered enough?" All I could hear was silence. The voice spoke no more.

The anger I experienced was so overwhelming. Sarah was the child I dreamed of and prayed for. She was also my last hope of conceiving a child that would have been my husband's. I could not comprehend why Sarah was taken from me. Was God punishing me for my past?

The night of the mission I was filled with so much hurt, anger, and pain that I was having difficulty letting all the emotions go and surrendering totally to God. When Father Izral laid his hands on my head and began to pray, I felt the Holy Spirit fill me with a tremendous warmth followed by unconditional peace. It was then I released all my feelings and emotions and began to cry out to God for forgiveness for lashing out at Him with anger. Through this experience I have learned that the miscarriage was an act of nature, not a punishment from God.

I know the tremendous suffering those who have had an abortion and/or a miscarriage experience feel because I, too, have been there. I have experienced the hurt, pain, depression, anger, condemnation, guilt, unforgiving of self, God and others and what I thought was betrayal from God. I know what it is like to fall to the pit of hell. But I also know how our loving God picked me up, took me in His arms, and held me with more love than I have ever experienced in my life.

A Visionary Visits St. Margaret Mary Church

A visionary from Australia, who receives apparitions from the Blessed Mother and Jesus, came to St Margaret Mary church in 1995. She travels around the world speaking about the two hearts (the Sacred Heart of Jesus and the Immaculate Heart of Mary). She has the approval of her Bishop.

Before attending Mass and hearing the visionary speak, I asked the Lord what His will was for me and to tell me during the evening. When I heard the visionary speak, I would cry off and on trying to grasp every word. When she spoke of the "victim soul" a strong sense, came over me. I then thought of my vision of heaven with Jesus and all the babies. His words rang out in my head, "You will suffer much. You must die to yourself and die for me." When I heard this for the first time, I did not totally understand what He meant until I heard about the "victim soul". I began to cry uncontrollably.

Jesus said, "Fear not, for I am with you. You have been chosen to die for the aborted babies in heaven and all those who have experienced abortion – the mothers, fathers, and family members. Also, the doctors, nurses, and worker assistants and all who have hardened their hearts. Through your suffering and death, they will be saved and you will be with Me in paradise."

Then Our Blessed Lady told me that my mission is to continue to *do what God the Father has called me to do.* The last part of my mission that God is calling me to is a deeper suffering, a suffering that is excruciating. At times the pain will grow unbearable. Just know St. Therese and I are with you. Turn to us and we will give you the strength and courage to carry out the will of God. Jaqualene and I went off to the side to share our messages with each other. As we were reading them a beautiful butterfly kept landing on the messages and us. We believed Our Lady was affirming what we heard and telling us a new life in Christ was to begin.

On October 25, 1996, we were sitting in the cemetery in Medjugorje. When I looked up at the cross on top of Cross Mountain, it began to spin, disappear, and all of a sudden Our Blessed lady appeared to me. I told her I accept the deeper suffering with joy, but to stay close to me because I am a wimp and have a low tolerance of pain. She told me she was not going to leave me and she has kept her word.

When we arrived at San Giovanni, Fr. Joseph, a Capuchin Monk that lives there, took us on a tour. I snapped pictures of everything. Something Fr. Joseph said to us pierced my heart. He said, "Padre Pio suffered tremendously, in silence, and without consolation." It was sitting before Padre Pio's tomb that the words played over and over in my mind. Then I heard Padre Pio say, "My gift to you will manifest in a picture you took in this place. Just know I love you and I am with you."

When we arrived home I got the pictures of the trip developed. When I looked through the San Giovanni pictures, there was my gift from Padre Pio. The picture of his room or cell had his face in it. I began to cry and cry. What a blessing!

The most important things I have learned about suffering is that when we suffer in silence and without consolation, we ease the sufferings of Our Lord Jesus Christ. This brought me great joy. The other thing was that the more we suffer for our salvation and others, the more we grow in holiness and perfection. We are then totally purified. Through Padre Pio I have also learned to lift my sufferings up in union with Jesus' sufferings and for the Glory of God. "Silence is golden."

Chapter 3
Fr. Richard Carroll
JESUS IS LORD

The disciple of Christ must not only keep the faith and live on it, but also profess it, confidently bear witness to it, and spread it: ... 'So every one who acknowledges me before men, I also will acknowledge before my Father who is in heaven; but whoever denies me before men, I also will deny before my Father who is in heaven.'" (Matthew 10:32-33)[x]
(Catechism of the Catholic Church)

"In the revealed text it is the Heavenly Father himself who comes to us in love and who dwells with us, disclosing to us the nature of his only begotten Son and his plan of salvation for humanity."[xi]
*(Pope John Paul, II * Tertio Millennio Adventiente)*

Author's Note: In order to understand a little better the Friday night talk that I gave, I would like to give you an overview of our journey to the Father at St. Margaret Mary Church. This will help the reader to understand some of the steps that God the Father has taken to prepare us for the Triumph of the Immaculate Heart of Mary; and the return to God the Father. In the chapters that follow our retreat talks, I will try to tie it all together for you. You will then realize that role that God the Father plays in bringing his children home. These are the more significant events in the life of our parish.

The Outline of Our Journey as a Parish
1. December 18, 1983 – Perpetual Adoration began – beginning of the Remnant Church.
2. December 31, 1989 – First book published – *A Priest Looks at Medjugorje* – went three times to Medjugorje.
3. 1993 – Published *The Remnant Church*.
4. March 14, 1994 – 1200 signed up to board the Ark of the Covenant. They all went to confession that night.

Mary is known in the church as the Ark of the Covenant – A repentant community.

5. 1996 – Published third book *The Third Millennium: The Triumph of Our Lady* – The emphasis' is on Divine Mercy.
6. April 1996 – Intercessory Prayer meeting on Friday night begins.
7. 1997-1998 – Homes enthroned with the picture of Jesus as Divine Mercy. These are the final days of Divine Mercy —then Divine Justice.
8. June 4-6, 1999 – Parish Jubilee Retreat – **A Journey to the Father.**
9. August 1, 1999 – Sunday – **Celebrating God the Father of all Nations.**

It will also help you to see the whole picture when you have an overview of the retreat itself. If you can imagine this Journey to the Father as a map, all of us have a small piece of that treasured map. Each of us in the Christian community will play a part in facilitating this journey. If you fail to share your piece of the map, we will all be lost.

Retreat Outline

1. Alan Fries – Childlike submission.
2. Linda Jefferson, Ted Besh, Toni Hernandez – suffering. The cross is integral to the journey to the Father.
3. Deacon Weber, Beverly Fisher – The role of the Holy Spirit.
4. Bernie McClelland and Fr. Mossy Gallagher – The Eucharist – Intimacy with Jesus
5. Dr. Mike and Helen Rozeluk – Healing – A sign on the way.
6. Fr. Carroll – Jesus is Lord, The Role of Mary, and The Priesthood.

In order to appreciate fully the Friday night talk, Jesus is Lord, it is important to realize that God the Father intends to bring the entire Christian church together. I have no idea how he will accomplish this. But I know the prayer of Jesus will not be wasted. Christ prayed: "Father I pray that they all may be one, as you are in me and I in you, that they all may be one in us."

Those Catholic Christians, who became involved in the charismatic movement, learned a tremendous amount from our Pentecostal brothers and sisters. The Catholic Church will always be indebted to them. I acknowledge that I have benefited much from studying the work of Dr. Bill Bright. I have read the work of Dr. Bill Bright about campus crusade. I had learned much about evangelization from his video series.

The sorrow in my heart, is the same sorrow I believe God the Father feels for those Catholics who have abandoned their faith due to involvement in Campus Crusade and Pentecostalism. The apostasy that we see in the Catholic Church today is a clear sign to me, that God the Father is going to intervene. As you read 1 Thessalonians 5:1-4, you realize St. Paul the great evangelizer was trying to warn us to be prepared. St. Paul wrote: "As regards specific times and moments, brothers, we do not need to write you; you know very well that the day of the Lord is coming like a thief in the night. Just when people are saying 'peace and security,' ruin will fall on them in suddenness of pains overtaking a woman in labor, and there will be no escape. You are not in the dark, brothers, that the day should catch you off guard, like a thief."

Just as many of us have learned from Protestantism, I feel that our Protestant brothers and sisters have much to benefit, by studying the teachings of the Catholic Church. The fullness of the truth can be found in the Catholic Church particularly, the belief in the "real presence of Jesus, body and blood soul and divinity" in Holy Communion, love for Mary as our own mother and intercessory, and the doctrine of the Trinity.

Many Catholics who leave our church don't realize that they are giving up the precious presence of Christ that they have experienced since they were seven years old of becoming one with Jesus through Holy Communion. Like St. Paul we can say: "It is no longer I, it is Christ who live in me."

I was overwhelmed when 600-700 Catholics on successive nights proclaimed Jesus as Lord of their lives, and had a born-again experience. I can tell you not only these adults but hundreds of young people over the last 13 years have had this experience. The Holy Spirit taught us how to pray over people; and marvelous gifts have resulted. I was not privileged to study the theology of the born again experience in the seminary. But I certainly see no contradictions to our Catholic belief.

Years ago David Wilkerson wrote a book entitled *The Cross and the Switchblade*. He used an apt example of a born again experience. Many Christians can quote the bible, define the teachings of the Christ, but never seemed to have experienced its power and the presence of the Holy Spirit. Wilkerson compared religion to eating a steak. You may know all the characteristics of a steak ... it is a Kansas City beef, it is corn-fed beef, is there a great amount of marbling, etc. But put that steak on a grill and the aroma overwhelms you. The Holy Spirit is doing that for the church ... putting us on a grill and making Christianity desirable once again to God the Father's little ones.

Explanation of Mass of Inner Healing

After Holy Communion, during a Mass of inner healing the Blessed Sacrament is exposed. We have this healing Mass every first Friday of the month. The celebrant says the prayers for inner healing. Because the Blessed Sacrament is exposed, the final blessing is not given.

Occasionally, we conclude the Mass of Inner Healing with benediction and blessing with the monstrance. Instead of a simple blessing over the congregation we go throughout the church blessing the participants row by row. Many of us have experienced the healing touch of Jesus in the monstrance at the Catholic Charismatic Conference in New Orleans.

I saw one of our parishioners being healed of a serious back injury three years ago at a healing service at the Catholic Charismatic Conference. He was in severe pain for years. At that conference Fr. Tardiff, an internationally known priest-healer announced that someone was cured of a back injury. This parishioner has been pain free for three years.

The prayer teams are called forward after the completion of the prayers for Inner Healing. Then those who wish to be prayed over come to the foot of the altar. During the retreat, the prayer teams, together with the guests from Toronto, Dr. Mike and Helen Rozeluk, and myself, prayed over those who wished the infusion of the Holy Spirit as well as those who were praying for physical or spiritual healing.

Resting in the Spirit

Thirteen years ago, we embarked on this remarkable journey with the Holy Spirit, at a confirmation retreat in Mandeville, Louisiana. As soon as Fr. Lafranz prayed over these teens most of them fell over backwards. One of the adult men caught them and gently laid them on the carpet. But not everyone who is prayed over rests in the spirit. Despite the powerful prayers of many charismatic leaders, I can remember being slain in the spirit only once. Nevertheless something happens if we are open to the power of the Holy Spirit, even if we do not rest in the spirit.

If we are childlike, the Holy Spirit can work in our lives. He can use this prayer or anointing with oil to deeply touch us. Some gingerly fall backward and a catcher guides them to the floor. The Holy Spirit touches others even if they don't fall backwards, i.e. become slain in the Spirit. This is often called a born again experience when used in conjunction with the appropriate prayer.

I have learned to submit my will to that of God the Father. If he wants to use me by praying over people, I will do it. The results, if any, are up to God the Father.

Fr. Robert DeGrandis, S.S.J. has written a wonderful book entitled *Resting in the Spirit.* I have been present in a number of healing services done by Fr. DeGrandis and value his friendship as well as his wonderful work.

In the introduction to this work, DeGrandis makes a wonderful point that many priests and bishops who oppose "Resting in the Spirit", have never had an experience of the Holy Spirit. In this book, Fr. DeGrandis lets the people tell their own experience. It is a wonderful testimony to the power of the Holy Spirit.

Conclusion

On Friday night and again on Saturday night, Dr. Mike, Helen, the prayer teams and myself prayed over whomever wanted to come forward. On Friday night this lasted until 11:00 PM. The Mass had started at eight. Helen, Mike and I had a bread and butter sandwich and cup of Irish tea afterwards. We weren't hungry, though we had not eaten since noon.

On Saturday we concluded the service by praying over those who so desired. Many hundreds came forward...some didn't. The call itself is a gift of God the Father

"Born Again Experience"

Both on Friday and Saturday night during the Mass I had everyone present recite Fr. Stenzel's prayer for a born again experience. Fr. Stenzel is a Franciscan priest currently stationed at the Houma diocese retreat center. For years he had worked in evangelization in Detroit, Michigan. Fr. Stenzel developed this prayer to be used for Catholic Christians.

We had 10,000 prayers printed. On one side was the prayer on the other a picture of Divine Mercy. The purpose of this prayer, like that used by Campus Crusade, is to ask the Holy Spirit to make us born again Christian Catholics.

God the Father's Gift

It was a highlight of my 40 years in the priesthood to see hundreds of Catholics experience the presence of God through this prayer as well as by being prayed over at the end of the service. It was clearly a gift of God the Father, who loves all of his children, for them to experience the power of the Holy Spirit.

I know that God the Father loves his children in a special way. Each of you is his "beloved sons" or his "precious daughters." It was an extraordinary gift to me to have so many of his children leave St. Margaret Mary Church, knowing, in a most powerful way, that God loves each of them.

Are You Saved?

Millions of Roman Catholics are asked, "are you saved?" We have lost countless thousands to the Pentecostal Church because Catholics simply couldn't answer that question. The hundreds of Catholics who participated in our parish retreat can now answer that question.

We say to our Protestant brothers and sisters that we take seriously the warning of St. Paul: "... let anyone who thinks he is standing upright watch out lest he fall!"(1 Corinthians 10:12) Even Dr. Billy Graham admitted that in his early crusades he often used born again converts to be witnesses. But he found that if the new converts did not read the bible and go to church on Sunday, they would quickly fall away. Salvation is far more than mouthing a simple formula.

Those who attended our parish retreat know that they are saved. We know our salvation is due to the fact that we are aware that we are sinners, and Jesus Christ who suffered, died and rose from the dead has forgiven us.

We Catholics are so convinced that we are sinners, we go to confession regularly. Jesus gave his church the power to forgive sins when he told us through the apostles: "if you forgive men's sins, they are forgiven them; if you hold them bound, they are held bound."(John 20:23)

As Catholics we are reminded of our sinfulness every time we attend Mass. At the beginning of our services, we proclaim our sorrow for our sins. At St. Margaret Mary we have a huge crucifix behind the main altar. Recently, a Protestant visitor remarked that we must not believe in the resurrection since we do not have a "resurrected Christ." On the contrary, we certainly proclaim Jesus as resurrected in the Nicene Creed every Sunday. But the crucifix reminds each of us that we are sinners and that we are saved only by the power of the cross of Jesus Christ.

Finally, we proclaim Jesus as Lord through the power of the Holy Spirit. I know Jesus through faith and proclaim my belief in him in the Nicene Creed. This creed, said at Mass every Sunday, comes from the Council of Nicea in 325. It states that we believe in God the Father, in Jesus who was born of a virgin suffered died and rose again, and we believe in the Holy Spirit. This prayer we proudly proclaim every week.

Personal Relationship with Jesus Christ

Every Catholic has a personal relationship with Jesus Christ. We know Jesus by faith. The sacraments, as well as our reading of Holy Scripture, sustain our faith, passed on to us through baptism. The sacrament of confirmation we receive the fullness of the Holy Spirit which strengthens us in our relationship with Christ.

But Catholics have an advantage. We know Jesus intimately in the sacrament of Holy Eucharist. We receive his body and blood, soul and divinity whenever we receive Holy Communion worthily. As we are told in St. John's gospel 6:54: "He who feeds on my flesh and drinks my blood has life eternal and I will raise him up on the last day."

Our personal relationship with Jesus is reinforced by Perpetual Adoration. Jesus does not lie hidden in our tabernacle. Our monstrance containing the sacred host is adored 24 hours a day, 7 days a week. Since 1983 we have had Perpetual Adoration of the Blessed Sacrament. We spend all this time with Jesus because we know he is truly present in the Eucharist. That's a personal relationship with Christ.

Many Christian churches serve bread and grape juice during a service they call "communion". However if you ask the minister whether he believes this bread and wine is actually the body and blood of Jesus, he would say of course not, it is only a "memorial". It is the clear teaching of the Catholic Church that the Eucharist i.e. Holy Communion is the body and blood, soul and divinity of Jesus Christ. In order to have "communion," the church needs a priesthood, which most Protestants abhor.

In the new Catechism of the Catholic Church the teaching of the church is given: "The Council of Trent summarizes the Catholic faith by declaring: 'because Christ our Redeemer said that it was truly his body that he was offering under the species of bread, it has always been the conviction of the Church of God, and this holy Council now declares again, that by the consecration of the bread and wine there takes place a change of the whole substance of the bread into the substance of the body of Christ our Lord and of the whole substance of wine into the substance of his blood. This change the holy Catholic Church fittingly and properly called transubstantiation.'"[xii]

Again the Catechism says: "Christ is present whole and entire in each of the species and whole and entire in each of their parts, in such a way that the breaking of the bread does not divide Christ."[xiii] Protestants, who say we have "communion", should ask simply, "Is it Jesus we receive or is it simply bread?

I have heard the voice of Jesus knocking on my heart. But I have also heard the voice of his mother Mary calling me home to God the Father.

Our love for Mary reinforces our love for God the Father and for his son Jesus as well as the Holy Spirit. We are truly Trinitarians. We believe in the Trinity: Father, Son and Holy Spirit, three persons in one God. What a magnificent relationship we have to our God who is so near.

Proclamation

On Friday night and on Saturday night we as a Catholic Christian community proclaimed "Jesus is Lord." By the grace of the Holy Spirit and the love of God the Father we know we are saved. We are born again Christian Catholics. For this we will always be grateful.

From Divine Mercy Prayer Card

Lord, God, I confess that I am a sinner.
I confess that I need your Son Jesus.
Please forgive me in His Name.

Lord Jesus, I believe You died for me
And that You are alive and listening
To me now. I now turn from my sins and
Welcome You into my heart. Come and
Take control of my life. Make me the
Kind of person You want me to be.

Thank You for loving me, for forgiving
Me and for coming to live in my heart –
Never to leave me or forsake me.

Now, fill me with your Holy Spirit,
Who will show me how to live for you
And acknowledge You before men
As my Savior and my Lord.

I love You, Jesus. Amen.

****

Jesus is Lord!
Friday Night, June 4, 1999
Fr. Richard Carroll

I'm very grateful to Linda Jefferson for allowing me to read her testimony. Linda is quite ill and unable to be with us tonight. Each one of us has our own story to tell. Sometimes these stories are happy stories like Alan Fries telling you about seeing angels. I have to tell you that I'm a very jealous of him. Tomorrow you are going to hear stories about suffering from Ted Besh, who has been in a wheel chair for twenty years, after being a Delta pilot. Toni Hernandez will tell her story of the death of her precious little four year old who is certainly St. Margaret Mary's little saint. You're going to hear two testimonies about the power of the Holy Spirit from Deacon Weber and Beverly Fischer. Bernie McClleland and Father Gallagher will talk about their love for the Eucharist. Tomorrow at 3:30 PM Dr. Mike and Helen Rozeluk will share the story of Mike's healing and the number of people who have been healed because of the ministry God has given them.

I always tell young people when they give their testimony, that there is a great risk in doing it. We saw that happen about seven years ago. One of our young students from LSU was sharing a story of his conversion. He told how at LSU he became involved in drinking alcohol and smoking marijuana. While he was at LSU this young man had a conversion experience that was incredible. It was amazing to me to see a young person 21 years old talking about being a sinner; and God welcomed this young sinner home.

It was an incredible gift that he gave. The time that he told that story, our retreat team was giving a confirmation retreat for another parish. This parish celebrates confirmation in the 8th grade. It was a wonderful retreat.

The priests and teens prayed over everyone, as I hope every one of you will be prayed over either tonight or tomorrow night. The day after the retreat the pastor received a visit from a doctor's wife, who told him, "I don't want you ever to expose my son to a drug addict. I am so angry at you," she said, "that you put my child in this kind of situation." The result is that it will be a long time before the children of that parish will be allowed to be prayed over or be slain in the Spirit, as all of our children have been for 13 years. Incidentally I told the pastor the rest of the story that this young man went into the seminary the next summer. He was ordained a priest last June. We were privileged to have him say one of his first Masses at St Margaret Mary.

There is a risk that we all go through in sharing our testimonies. We ask you to be forgiving as God the Father forgave us. Listen not just to the words but listen with your hearts. That's how God the Father deals with his children. We got into this business of praying over children, and later as you know praying over adults, not because I wanted to do it. Fifteen years ago at a confirmation retreat in Mandeville, Father LaFranze was saying the closing Mass. Somehow, God just said to me, "ask Fr. LaFranze to pray over these teens." Incidentally, Fr. LaFranze died about three years ago.

After communion I said, "Father LaFranze is a very spirit filled priest. Anyone who wants to be prayed over can come forward and he will pray over you. If you don't want to, you don't have to." It was really funny, because I was in the chair just watching all of this and I remember one of the girls came up to me and asked, "Do you see what he is doing? One by one the students came forward to be prayed over by Fr. LaFranze and they gently fell backwards, resting in the spirit. A couple of adults acted as catchers and the students had a remarkable experience. I said, "No what is he doing?" She said, "He's pushing them over, and if they don't fall over, he's pushing them." "I think maybe your right." I said, "but don't come forward for prayer if you don't want to receive the infilling of the Holy Spirit." From then on our high school teens preparing for confirmation have enjoyed this spiritual experience.

I am convinced that our young adults need this powerful experience of the Holy Spirit. Many of them go to a secular college such as LSU. One of the first questions asked of them by members of Campus Crusade is: "Are you saved?" Most Catholics respond by saying: "I've never heard these words... I don't know."

Why? Because in the Catholic Church we are very mindful of the scriptures, where St. Paul says: "let anyone who thinks he is standing upright watch out lest he fall!"(1 Corinthians 10:12) So if anyone asks us if we are saved, we'll probably say, "I sure hope so."

The "born again experience" is a terminology developed by Dr. Bill Bright, founder of Campus Crusade. If you study the scriptures that Bill uses, you recognize that there's not one of these scriptures that you and I don't agree with. I will read them to you. You will see quite easily that as Catholics we agree with all of these texts.

First Spiritual Law

Dr. Bright said the first spiritual law is: "God loves you and offers a wonderful plan for your life."[xiv] "God so loved the world that He gave His one and only Son, that whoever believes in Him shall not perish but have eternal life."(John 3:16). How many of you know that God loves you. Raise you hands. It's amazing! You have all raised your hands.

Second Spiritual Law

Dr Bright's Second law is: "Man is **sinful** and **separated** from God. Therefore, he cannot know and experience God's love and plan for his life."[xv] "The wages of sin is death." (Roman 6:23)

51

How many of you really realize that you are sinners? Raise you hands. Good Lord, we got a pile of sinners here! I love when the late Bishop Sheen wrote "I thank God I am a sinner now I can have Jesus as my Savior"

Third Spiritual Law

The third spiritual law of Dr. Bright is: "Jesus Christ is God's **only** provision for man's sins. Through Him you can know and experience God's love and plan for your life." [xvi] Scripture tells us in St John's Gospel: "Jesus said to him, 'I am the way, and the truth, and the life; no one comes to the Father but through Me.'" (John 14:6). In another passage quoted by Dr Bright, "God demonstrates His own love toward us, in that while we were yet sinners, Christ died for us."(Romans 5:8) Are there any of you here tonight that does not accept the words of Jesus that He is "...the way, the truth, and the life"? I am glad you all agree.

How many of us realize that Jesus died for our sins? The entire congregation; that's wonderful. That's why we have that crucifix; with the corpus of Jesus behind our main altar. We all know it is through the cross of Jesus that we are saved. But Jesus also rose from the dead. How many of you accept that dogma of faith? Raise you hands! All of you are close to being saved. (Laughter fills the room)

Every Sunday we profess the Nicene Creed from the first general council in 325 AD, we proclaim that Jesus was born of a virgin, suffered, died and rose on the third day. This has been an essential tenet of our faith for nearly 1700 years

Fourth Spiritual Law

The final law of Dr. Bright is: "we must individually **receive** Jesus Christ as Savior and Lord; then we can know and experience God's love and plan for our lives."[xvii] Dr Bright uses four scriptural texts to illustrate this point.

a) We must receive Christ. "As many as received him, to them He gave the right to become children of God, even to those who believe in His name" (John 1:12).

b) We receive Christ through Faith. "By grace you have been saved through faith; and that not of yourselves, it is a gift of God; not as a result of work that no one should boast" (Ephesians 2:8,9).

c) When we receive Christ, we experience a new birth. (Read John 3:1-8).

d) We receive Christ through personal invitation. [Christ speaking] "Behold, I stand at the door and knock; if any one hears My voice and opens the door, I will come in to him." (Revelation 3:20)[xviii]

As we have seen, we profess our belief every Sunday in the Creed from the council of Nicene: We believe in God the Father, we believe in God the Son who was born of the Virgin Mary, suffered, died and rose, and we believe in the Holy Spirit. So as we receive Christ through faith, St. Paul says, "By grace you have been saved through faith..." and when you receive Christ, you experience a new birth.

Now here's the one text that Catholic's have to understand very clearly. In John 3:1-8 we're told no one can receive the Kingdom of God unless he's born again of water in the Holy Spirit. The first meaning of that text in Catholic theology is very clear. How are we reborn, by the sacrament of Baptism? If you reborn, you're reborn by baptism. Now when Dr. Bright is talking about is a secondary meaning of the scripture; that " born again" is a type of experience where we feel God's presence. It is an experience of the Holy Spirit.

Finally he said we receive Christ by personal invitation, and he quotes Revelation 3:20 "Behold, I stand at the door and knock; if any one hears My voice and opens the door, I will come in to him."[xix] The door handle is on the inside, when God knocks all you have to do is open.

After this Mass of inner healing (Friday night) and again following the Mass on Saturday night we are going to pray a prayer to become a "born again Catholic" We will say this prayer on Sunday as well.

I want you to experience the presence of God the Father. The prayer that we will use is on the back of the Divine Mercy picture. This prayer was written by Father Stenzel, and is similar to the prayer used by Campus Crusade and Dr. Bill Bright.

Dr. Bright's prayer is quite simple. In his brochure he explains this prayer as follows:

"The following explains how you can receive Christ: **You can receive Christ right now by Faith through prayer (prayer is talking with God.** God knows your heart and is not so concerned with your words as He is with the attitude of your heart. The following is a suggested prayer:
'Lord, Jesus, I need You. Thank You for dying on the cross for my sins. I open the door of my life and receive You as my Savior and Lord. Thank You for forgiving my sins and giving me eternal life. Take control of the throne of my life.
Make me the kind of person
You want me to be. [xx]

I believe that many of our children who have left God the Father's home could be welcomed back if they had this simple knowledge on this simple little card. "The Catholic born again experience" of Fr Dwayne Stenzel. From now on, when anybody says to you. "Are you born again?" You can say, "Absolutely, I am a born again Catholic Christian." But you know what, not only do I have a personal relationship to Jesus through faith, but I've got something more than that. I have a personal relationship with Jesus by receiving His body and blood in the Eucharist. Jesus said in John 6:54: "he who feeds on my flesh and drinks my blood has life eternal..." I do that every time I receive Holy Communion worthily.

Another way we experience our personal relationship with Jesus Christ is through Perpetual Adoration of the Blessed Sacrament. Since December 1983 we have spent every hour of every day adoring Jesus' presence in the Eucharist. What a gift this is to the entire Church!

Not only do I have a personal relationship through faith as you Protestants do, and through the Eucharist, but I know that I have a special relationship with God the Father because I love the Mother of Jesus. I will tell you one thing from my experience and the experience of everyone in the church of St Margaret Mary, if you love Mary, the mother of Jesus there is no way you can't love Jesus, or have a personal relationship with him. All of you are truly BORN AGAIN CATHOLIC CHRISTIANS. AMEN?

AND THE ENTIRE CONGREGATION THAT NIGHT REPLIED AMEN!

Chapter 4
Abandonment to the Providence of God the Father

"Jesus asks for childlike abandonment to the providence of our heavenly Father who takes care of his children's smallest needs: 'Therefore do not be anxious, saying, 'What shall we eat?' Or 'What shall we drink?'...Your heavenly Father knows that you need them all. But seek first his kingdom and his righteousness, and all these things shall be yours as well'" (Matthew 6:31-33)[xxi]
(Catechism of the Catholic Church)

"The first year, 1997, will be devoted to reflection on Christ, the Word of God, made man by the power of the Holy Spirit. ...In the revealed text it is the Heavenly Father himself who comes to us in love and who dwells with us, disclosing to us the nature of his only begotten Son and his plan of salvation for humanity"[xxii]
*(Pope John Paul, II * Tertio Millennio Adventiente)*

Author's Note: You are going to read about two extraordinary stories of suffering. Toni Hernandez is going to share her testimony about the death of her four-year old child Katie. She is St. Margaret Mary Church's parish saint.

Following her story you will experience a different kind of cross. Ted Besh was a young pilot. He had everything going for him, a beautiful wife, six gorgeous and gifted children and an exciting career as a Delta pilot. Their stories illustrate the point that the cross of Jesus Christ comes in different forms and shapes.

The story of Katie touched our entire community. When I learned that she was dying, I was approached by someone who reminded me that Pope Pius X, the man who lowered the age for reception of first communion from 12 to 7 or the "age of reason." This holy pontiff had allowed a four-year old, who was dying to receive the Eucharist. The child must know that it is Jesus she is receiving. When I questioned Katie there was no doubt in my mind that she was ready for this sacrament.

My most endearing moment with Katie came when she was close to death. She received communion almost every day, after making her First Holy Communion. One day after I had given Katie communion, her mother looked at this dying child and said to her: "Katie, Father Carroll seems especially sad today. Would you give him a hug?" At that time the arms of this child was the size of my fingers. She was in intense pain. She lifted herself up and wrapped those precious arms around me. I knew I had been hugged by a saint. It was very hard to keep from letting her see the tears that were coming down my cheeks.

If you ever visit St Margaret Mary church you will see a huge window in the chapel which depicts the Triumph of the Immaculate Heart of Mary. It is Mary crushing the head of the serpent (Revelations 12). The angel next to Our Lady is Katie.

There will soon be a statue of another saint called Blessed Imelda. Imelda is the patroness of first communicants. This statue will be on a side altar with Our Lady. They will stand under a mosaic of St Michael the archangel. A host in this scene is to remind us that this young Dominican nun died at age 11, in ecstasy when she was allowed to receive Holy Communion a year earlier than her peers. That statue will always remind me of our own Eucharistic saint- Katie Hernandez.

****

The Story of Katie Hernandez
By: Toni Hernandez

I would like to begin with a prayer. In the name of the Father and of the Son and the Holy Spirit. Amen. Come Holy Spirit enlighten my heart to see the things that are from God. Come Holy Spirit into my mind that I may know the things that are from God. Come Holy Spirit into my soul that I may only belong to God. Sanctify all that I think, say, and do, that all will be for the Glory of God, Amen.

First let me say, this is not a talk about sadness or grief, rather it's a talk about hope, great joy and the workings of Mercy on those who put their trust in God.

I do not want you to think that our cross is any heavier than yours. Many of you have lost loved ones and others here carry heavy burdensome crosses of your own. God blesses each and every one of us with Grace and shows us His great love as we carry our crosses daily.

Katie is the fourth of six children that my husband, Lou and I were blessed with. When Katie was only a week old I noticed some purplish spots on her skin and her lymph node under her arm was enlarged. I knew something was wrong. After telling Lou about it I called to make an appointment to see Katie's doctor. She saw Katie that morning and sent us to see a dermatologist to have some biopsies done. I didn't want to believe that something serious was wrong with Katie but I suspected something was.

Early that afternoon Katie's doctor called and said that she was coming over to talk to Lou and I. When she got to our home she told us what we didn't want to hear, that Katie had some form of cancer. She made arrangements for us to admit Katie to Children's Hospital in New Orleans. After Katie's doctor left the house, Lou and I were crying and Lou looked at me and said "we have to trust God." Lou got on the phone and made arrangements for Katie to be baptized. Deacon Vicroy came to our home and baptized Katie and then Lou, Katie, and I left for Children's Hospital. It took time before Katie was diagnosed with a severe form of leukemia. After 4 years of intense chemotherapy, multiple surgeries, including the removal of a metastatic brain tumor, a bone marrow transplant, and brief periods of remission, Katie died.

I would like to tell you a little bit about Katie. She was a very extraordinary child. She suffered very quietly and never complained about her illness. She was very stoic. It is very hard for me to explain what kind of child Katie was. She was always so good and so very loving. She was very spiritual and had great love for the Lord and the Blessed Mother. At the age of two she knew how to pray the rosary. We always felt like we had a piece of Heaven with us. I often thought is this child really human or an angel from God? There are only a few people in this parish that knew Katie well and appreciated these qualities in her. She brought such a great sense of peace and love to everyone she was with.

Over the 4 years of Katie's life Lou and I constantly prayed for a healing for Katie. Since the first time Lou said to trust God we never stopped trusting Him. Lou is the spiritual backbone of our family and always kept us focused on God through Katie's illness. We knew that what ever happened to Katie was God's will and we always accepted that. I don't want you to think that we were never angry with God or never questioned His will. We did a lot of that. It was very hard to see such a young child suffer so very much. But through the anger and many prayers always comes our surrender to God's Will.

Not only were Lou and my prayers continuous for Katie, but also were the prayers of many of the parishioners of this parish and other parishes in the area and our priests. Without them my family could not have gotten through the loss of Katie. I have learned over the years that it is only the Grace we receive from God, through the intercession of Our Lady, from prayers and the Sacraments that sustain us during the trails of this life. This Grace gives us peace and hope, and that it did for us.

You could always see the hand of God working in our lives, in the lives of the people of this parish and in Katie's life during her illness. A few weeks before Katie's death, a parishioner who is so dear to my family went to Father Carroll to see if Katie could receive Holy Communion. Father was reminded of Pope Pius X giving communion to a dying 4-year-old almost a century ago. Katie would go to daily Mass with me when she was well enough and we always sat in the first pew in the chapel. She knew that our Lord was present in the Blessed Sacrament. Father Carroll decided to allow Katie to received the Sacraments of the Eucharist and Confirmation at our home with Family and friends from church. When it came time for Katie to received her First Communion, Lou and I were very nervous and I know Father Carroll was also. I was holding Katie and Father Carroll thought that it would make Katie feel more comfortable if I gave her communion but she whispered in my ear and told me she wanted Father Carroll to give her communion. This was one of the many ways Katie showed Father Carroll how much she cared for him. It was truly a sight to behold because all of us that were close to Katie were aware of the fact that she knew she was receiving the Body, Blood, Soul and Divinity of Jesus Christ. How we all thanked God for blessing us with that moment. Katie was so blessed to receive communion almost daily until her death.

A couple of days before Katie died she was in a great deal of pain. Any movement she made was very painful.

All of a sudden she had a great smile on her face and she started reaching in the air like she was trying to grab for something. She wasn't talking very much at that point and couldn't tell me what she was seeing. I truly felt in my heart that she was seeing the Blessed Mother, and/or angels, and was trying to touch them. Later that day when I walked into my room to check on her I was overwhelmed with the smell of incense. Our faith was strong enough to move mountains and we knew that God could heal her, but at that moment I realized that a physical healing was not part of God's plan for Katie. You see, Lou and I had consecrated Katie to the Immaculate Heart of Mary when we took Katie to Medjugorje a year before her relapse. So the incense I smelled in the room that day was a little reminder of the offering we had made one year previously, the offering of Katie.

A few hours before Katie died I was lying next to her. Both Lou and I were so physically and mentally exhausted. In fact I remember telling Jaynell Weber at some point that I couldn't pray anymore and Jaynell told me that's what they were there for, to pray in our place. Katie became unresponsive and we knew it would be anytime before God would take her. Lou and I felt like our hearts were being ripped from our chests. It's really hard to explain how intense that pain is. I remember closing my eyes and thinking of Our Lady at the foot of the cross and telling her that I knew the pain Lou and I were feeling was less than a fraction of the pain she must have felt seeing her Son suffer and die such a horrible death. At that moment I knew that the only way Our Lady could have physically survived that ordeal was due to the singular grace she obtained from her total trust and abandonment to the Father's will.

On reading an article in the April 1999 Clarion Herald on the mystery of suffering the Holy Father, Pope John Paul II said, "Human suffering is a mystery that challenges Christians to place complete trust in God's plan, which may not always be grasped by human understanding. "Divine revelation helps us understand that suffering is not desired by God, but has entered the world because of sin. God allows suffering for the very salvation of man, drawing good out of evil." The Pope said that faith is needed to accept the fact of suffering along with the good that life offers. He continued: "The plans of God do not always coincide with human plans; they are infinitely better, but often remain incomprehensible to the human mind. Knowing that God loves us, we should place our trust in His Fatherly care, especially in the more difficult situations in our lives."

As Lou and I and our family walked the path with Katie that God gave us we had hope, peace, and felt great love from God and our spiritual family here at St. Margaret Mary Church. We always knew that God was in control and that all that was happening was His will and therefore, good would come of it. We stayed focused on that during the rough times and the wonderful times we had with Katie. Thanks to Lou's strong faith and total trust in God our whole family grew in faith from his example.

There are two prayers which were immensely comforting to Lou and I during Katie's illness and which we continue to pray frequently, one being the Memorare and the other is a prayer that I will close with. This prayer can be found in Blessed Faustina's diary and in most of the pamphlets on devotion to Divine Mercy. It is a suggested prayer to be said at the 3 o'clock hour. So let us close with that prayer:

Eternal Father, in whom Mercy is endless and the treasury of compassion inexhaustible. Look kindly upon us and increase Your Mercy in us, that in difficult moments we may not despair nor become despondent, but with great confidence submit ourselves to your Holy Will which is Love and Mercy itself. Amen.

****

Ted Besh
From Cockpit to Wheelchair

Author's Note: The story of Ted Besh is an inspiration for all of us in St Margaret Mary parish. For someone as active as Ted was as a pilot, to be forced into a wheelchair is an unbelievable cross.

I have known Ted and Imelda from my first days in Slidell. Ted and I used to play tennis together. I was always impressed with the strenuous efforts he made to keep in shape. I remember Ted playing tennis with me one day when it was so foggy you couldn't see the ball crossing the net.

Not only did I admire Ted, I am sure I was quite jealous of him when we first met. This young man had the courage of his convictions. At a time when Catholics routinely practiced birth control, He and Imelda had six young children. Ted seemed to have everything. Yet the cross he was given, took an enormous amount of courage to carry.

The strength of Ted Besh comes from his lovely wife Imelda. When Imelda was pregnant for Stephen, the doctor discovered she had RH factor. Many doctors would have had her abort the fetus. The doctor explained to Imelda and Ted that she could die in childbirth. But the faith of Imelda and the fact that she had a good Catholic doctor, allowed her to bring this child to term. Because of her deep faith this child was born healthy.

****

We Roman Catholic Christians do not believe there is an easy way in life if we really mean to follow the Lord. We may pray for healing and deliverance and in some cases relief of those sorts follow prayerful requests. But we realize there is value in bearing our cross. We believe we can unite our sufferings with those of Christ and much will be merited by that act.

We very much believe the statement of Jesus quoted in the Gospel of Luke 9:23 where he says: "Whoever wishes to be my follower must deny his very self, take up his cross each day, and follow in my steps."

I have been carrying a particularly demanding cross for over 21 years now. I am paralyzed more or less from the waist down. I never wanted to be. I can't walk or jog anymore. I didn't want to end up that way. I did not want this cross. But it is mine. How did I get to this point? What does it all mean? What have been the positive results of keeping on keeping on as we say in the rehabilitation business?

Here is how I got this way. The day after Thanksgiving of 1977 I was riding a 10 speed bicycle near Slidell for exercise. I was an airline pilot with Delta Airlines and I was due to go out on another flight as a copilot of a DC-8 aircraft on Sunday, two days in the future. I never made that flight. In 90 days or so I planned to go up to Atlanta to the Delta training center and begin training for my move up to captain on DC-9 aircraft. That never happened either.

Airline pilots are required to pass stringent physical exams every 6 months after they become captains. So I was attempting to be in the best shape possible for my anticipated new position. I got into bike riding because I had slightly injured an Achilles tendon jogging. I found I could get plenty of exercise on a bike without aggravating the injury. I got to the point where I would ride 20 to 30 miles an outing. This particular day I was passing the 20-mile point of a 25-mile ride. I had ridden around the eastern side of Slidell. I went from our home near John Slidell park all the way out to highway 90 and the location of the old White Kitchen restaurant that some old timers would be familiar with. I proceeded down 90 to the

Rigolets. Then I turned back toward Slidell on Salt Bayou road or La. 433.

Something told me I should stop at the little bridge that crosses Salt Bayou and phone my family from the bar by the bridge. But I didn't listen to that little voice. And I never made it to the interstate. About a mile before getting there I was struck from the rear by a van going at a high speed. The highway patrol figured it was going at least 55 mph when it struck me. The van was driven by a young man 18 years old, a tenth grade dropout who was intoxicated on alcohol and possibly marijuana. I was knocked about 120 feet down the roadway. My bike apparently fell on its side and turned into a sort of sled. I felt as though it never would stop sliding.

Initially as I was struck I felt a smooth although very forceful push. An instant later I was flying through the air about waist high, I would imagine. At this point the almost silly thought struck me that so far things weren't too bad. But that was followed immediately by the thought they were about to get a lot worse. And it happened ... as I hit the pavement I felt my body go numb from the waist down. I knew I had broken my back and had incurred some degree of spinal cord injury.

The van stopped about 10 or so feet behind me and the driver got out saying he did not think I was injured all that bad. He attempted to assist me to my feet. I told him not to touch me and to call an ambulance. The highway patrol officer investigating the accident wrote it up as a potential fatality. He knew how serious my situation was.

When I got to the hospital emergency room, I was met by a doctor with whom I used to play tennis.. He got me stabilized and into an ambulance. My wife, Imelda was called and she went with me to the hospital.

From Slidell we went to Ochsner hospital., the same night. The following evening it was necessary for the doctors to perform surgery. They had wanted to wait a few days and let the injury stabilize but I was bleeding internally and any further delay would be very dangerous. I was not aware of all this at the time. Imelda was however.

During surgery the doctors discovered my back was basically shattered at the base of my rib cage. In fact, the prognosis was so bleak the doctors told Imelda later that I might not even be able to sit up and get in a wheelchair. They placed steel rods in my back to hold things together. This was a tremendous jolt for my wife. Imelda was a young mother whose children ranged in age from 6 to 17. She had a difficult cross to bear..

A few days later our second oldest daughter came to visit me in intensive care. She was so shocked by the sights and smells of ICU that she fainted on the way out and broke her jaw. So she had to be admitted for surgery. Imelda did not tell me about that until sometime later. How she took all of that I don't know. She is an unbelievable person of great faith with a serene and accepting spirit. Those characteristics allowed her to bear up under this great load.

When you are first injured so severely you wonder if you want to live at all. I felt I needed to find a reason to stay around before embarking on a rehabilitation program. The doctors assured me I was putting the cart before the horse. They said I needed to learn the basics about how to live with the injury and I would find many interesting things to do with my life sooner than I then realized. It turned out they were right.

Six months of rehabilitation followed in Jackson, Mississippi. It felt like boot camp in the Marine corps. The therapists would push us so hard and we would feel like shouting at them to lay off. We called our workout room "The Pain Room."

What did it all mean? I had flown jet aircraft for 21 years by that time and had rung up 10,000 accident free flight hours in the Air Force and with Delta Airlines. To be felled by a bicycle seemed ludicrous. An experience in intensive care seemed to explain a part of what was happening.

A couple of days after surgery I was laying in a Stryker frame steel bed in intensive care relaxing under the effects of pain killing drugs. I found I was hallucinating. I would see scenes reminiscent of looking into the sky when I was on my back. Every two hours the nurses would turn the frame over and I would be looking down. At those times I would see scenes similar to those you see when looking down from a plane or from a high mountain or things you would see when scuba diving and looking down at the sea floor. It was all very entertaining.

Once I was face down and looking into what appeared to be an old fashioned well found on many farms sixty years ago. This kind of well t used to have the hand crank that pulled up a bucket of cold water on the end of a long rope. The well appeared to be about five feet across. It looked to be about ten to twenty feet deep. I recall seeing a little bright light about the size of a nickel at the bottom of the well. At the time I had the feeling as though a giant bear had me by the back and would not let go. This was very uncomfortable and I felt as though I was in prison. I was very angry about it. So I started talking to God about what I was feeling. I told Him I thought it was mean for Him to give me this feeling of imprisonment just after allowing me to be run over by a drunk. My family had almost lost a husband and a father. I would probably never walk again. And now I was made to feel as though a giant bear clutched me in its claws or jaws.

A voice spoke back to me out of the little light. It told me that I had a problem with my relationship with God and that was the cause of the ugly feeling in my back. The voice said I did not realize I was just a creature of God and He was first and always must be. I must remember that He made me and I was His son. In short, I needed to develop a spirit of submission, obedience, and humility if I expected life to improve. The voice told me to put God first in my life and the feeling of entrapment would go away. I told the Person in the light that I would never be able to fly again. It said He had not decided that yet. I said it would never be the same if I flew again; I would try to live for God this time more than I had before. He said nothing. Then He said I would never have to worry about anything. Whatever I needed I would have. The implication was that I would be provided for financially, but if I ever wanted a job or needed one just pray and ask and it would be forthcoming. I had always worried a lot about everything. I was made to realize I didn't need to do that any more. All my needs would be taken care of. At one point the voice said, "I am God and you are Ted. As soon as you get that relationship straight things are going to really brighten up for you and you will not have the feelings of entrapment and you will experience very little pain."

So I gave in. I told God I knew I was only a creature and He was the creator and that everything we have comes from Him. And almost immediately the bad feelings went away. And I had a peace about the situation. And I have pretty much had that peace every since.

I dearly loved flying. I hated to leave the cockpit. My feelings about flying are very well expressed by the poem High Flight. I have it written down here in my notes but I don't know if I can read it without breaking out into tears. Some of you may have read or heard of the poem in the past. It tells of the sheer thrill of flying high performance aircraft in God's great sky. I had flown jet trainer and fighter aircraft in the Air Force and had literally just gotten all over the sky on some of those flights. We used to do loops and rolls and high speed dives one after the other on training missions, pulling high g loads the whole while. Sometimes we did these maneuvers while flying in formation. I know of few greater thrills in life.

High Flight

Oh, I have slipped the surly bonds of earth
And danced the skies on laughter-silvered wings;
Sunward I've climbed and joined the tumbling mirth
Of sun-split clouds and done a hundred things
You have not dreamed of – wheeled and soared and swung
High in the sunlit silence. Hovering there
I've chased the shouting wind along and flung
My eager craft through footless halls of air
Up, up the long delirious, burning blue
I've topped the wind-swept heights with easy grace
Where never lark, or even eagle soared
And, while with silent lifting mind I've trod
The untrespassed sanctity of space
Put out my hand, and touched the face of God.

By: John Gillespie Magee, Jr.

On many flights both in the Air Force and with Delta I was privileged to see beautiful sights in nature that almost bedazzled my mind. This was especially true the last couple years I flew. I don't know if God was giving me a helping of beauty and His grandeur that was to have to last me for a lifetime or what. I have often wondered if I had been given a premonition of coming events when I was allowed to have those intense experiences of the beauty of His creation.

At the time of the accident we had six children in school. Kathleen was about to graduate from Slidell High School. Angela, the youngest, was in the first grade here at St. Margaret Mary School. Laura and Elaine were one and

69

two years behind Kathleen at Slidell High. Stephen was in his last year at St. Margaret Mary and John was in the fourth grade here.

So Imelda and I (especially Imelda) had a great load to carry. We were fortunate that I was able to return home in fairly good condition. She did not have to go to work so there were two of us at home when school was out for many years. The Besh kids were certainly not latch-key kids.

Our children responded to the challenges imposed on them by having a father who was disabled. They were very helpful to me in so many little ways. And they seemed to have made the same decision John, our youngest son once articulated. He said he never wanted to grow up to be like the young man who struck his father. He did not want to get involved in drugs or to abuse alcohol. He did not want to be a dropout. I never heard the others say it, but I am sure they felt the same.

They all responded by applying themselves in school and with extracurricular activities.   They all became educated and trained in some particular field .They all have become accomplished in their field. So today we have a cardiac rehabilitation nurse, a doctor, a high school teacher, an elementary school teacher, a daughter accomplished in computer work, and an award winning chef who served his country as a marine in a foxhole on the Kuwait border during Desert Storm. And that young marine, named John was a Eucharistic minister who made Holy Communion available to his comrades in the desert. He carried the eucharist all the way to Kuwait City through all those burning oil well fires. And John said he got so close to the Eucharist he did not want to give it back to the chaplain when the fight was over.

Five of our children have married and have presented us with seven grandchildren. All of our children have continued to be close to the Lord. And the young parents are raising their children to know God.

So God has required me to carry a cross. And He has allowed great blessings to result. I am sure many of the blessings have flowed from the simple fact of my trying to remain faithful and trying to stay the course when it would have been so easy to despair.

Matthew 6:31-33 says: "Stop worrying, then over questions like, 'What are we to eat, or what are we to drink, or what are we to wear?' The unbelievers are always running after these things. Your heavenly Father knows all that you need. Seek first His kingship over you, His way of holiness, and all these things will be given you besides."

I am sure what this passage says is true. I back slide at times. I am very human and it is difficult to always keep the right attitude. It was much easier just after the injury. I had a very close brush with death and that thought was in my mind just about all the time. But as time passes its easy to become lax and feel as though I had a right to all the blessings all along. I know that is not true. I know my family and I have been truly blessed. God made a tremendous promise to me and it has been more than fulfilled. Carrying this cross has been more than worth it. Great blessings have flowed from Imelda and I carrying that cross.

Chapter 5
Holy Spirit

"To believe in the Holy Spirit is to profess that the Holy Spirit is one of the persons of the Holy Trinity, consubstantial with the Father and the Son: 'with the Father and the Son he is worshiped and glorified'"
(nicene creed) "The Holy Spirit is at work with the Father and the Son from the beginning to the completion of the plan for our salvation."[xxiii]

(Catechism of the Catholic Church)

"For her part the church 'seeks but a solitary goal: to carry forward the work of Christ himself under the lead of the Holy Spirit, the Paraclete. And Christ entered this world to give witness to the truth, to rescue and not to sit in judgment, to serve and not to be served.'"[xxiv]

(Pope John Paul, II * Tertio Millennio Adventiente)

Author's Note: Anyone who attends Mass at St. Margaret Mary on Sunday or Intercessory Prayer on Friday night is impressed with a sense of the presence of the Holy Spirit.

Because of this childlike spirit, many of our parishioners are aware of the power of the Holy Spirit in their own lives. It is my hope that the testimonies of Beverly Fisher and Deacon John Weber will open you to the power of the Holy Spirit.

I believe this community has experienced enormous signs because the Holy Spirit wants to use all of you in a very powerful way. The reason that we have arrived at this stage of grace goes back to my sabbatical in 1987 when I visited Medjugorje.

The more I read about our Blessed Mother's warning and the more I read St. Paul's letter to the Romans, it becomes clear to me that we are dealing with the power of evil that is Satan himself. What better way to fight the evil one than by the power of the Holy Spirit.

Our own time seems to conform to the time which St. Paul in his letter talks about as the "day of wrath" or the "day of the Lord". That era of time could be a frightening period. This is why it is important that the Holy Spirit be very real in the lives of all of us. This is what St. Paul says in Romans: "I am not ashamed of the gospel. It is the power of God leading everyone who believes in it to salvation,..."(Romans 1:16)

You would weep if you knew how many people are ashamed of the gospel today. We know that since 1960 only 30 % of our Catholic people go to church regularly on Sunday. Only 37 % believe in the real presence of Jesus in the Eucharist according to the Gallup poll.

Ralph Martin has an excellent article in the New Covenant Magazine entitled "New Springtime or Chastisement? What is the spirit saying?" Mr. Martin says:
"There seems to be two major prophetic streams flowing in the Catholic Church today. The main spokesperson for the first is Pope John Paul II, who emphasizes the imminence of a new springtime, a new Pentecost, a Jubilee that consists of an encounter with God, a manifestation of Christ, an outpouring of the spirit.

"The main spokesperson for the second is Mary, the mother of Jesus, speaking through a multitude of apparitions. Some of her major themes are the urgency of the times, the imminence of warning, followed by a chastisement or judgement possibly involving war and natural disasters and the importance of turning to God.

"People who are trying to be open to the Spirit are sometimes puzzled by these seemingly contradictory themes. Of course, the Pope also speaks of the dangers of the times, the culture of death and other negative features, but his emphasis is in another direction. And Mary, of course, speaks often of God's mercy, goodness, grace and love, but in a context of urgency and a framework of heaven and hell, of temporal and eternal consequences for neglecting the mercy of God."[xxv]

Ralph Martin maintains that, "these two messages may be more profoundly in harmony than they appear at first sight"[xxvi]

Later in the article Martin goes on to say: "The pope made clear that preparation for the Great Jubilee of the year 2000 needs to involve a fundamental encounter with God." Pope John Paul "...speaks of this time of preparation ... as a 'new time of advent, at the end of which, like two thousand years ago, 'every man will see the salvation of God' (Lk. 3:6, Cf.Is 40:5)" ... an event which should recall to everyone and as it were make present anew the coming of the Word in the fullness of time ... In the time leading up to the third millennium after Christ, while 'the Spirit and the bride say to the Lord Jesus: Come!' this prayer of theirs is filled, as always, with an eschatological significance, which is also destined to give fullness of meaning to the celebration of the Great Jubilee. ... But at the same time *this prayer is directed toward a precise moment of history* that highlights the 'fullness of time' marked by the year 2000. The church wishes to *prepare* for this Jubilee *in the Holy Spirit*, just as the Virgin of Nazareth in whom the Word was made flesh was prepared by the Holy Spirit."[xxvii]

Ralph Martin quotes our Holy Father. "'... *that new springtime of Christian life* which will be revealed by the Great Jubilee, if Christians are docile to the actions of the Holy Spirit. ... As the third millenium of the redemption draws near, God is preparing a great springtime for Christianity, and we can already see its first signs.'"[xxviii]

Mary's Role in the Millennium

"Beginning at Fatima in 1917", Martin says, "and continuing throughout the century, Mary has come to warn of great dangers affecting the whole world, and the urgent need to take seriously the Gospel, to believe and repent."[xxix]

Martin traces the role of Our Lady in this century. "At Fatima, she warned of the spread of communism and the coming of World War II - unless there was sufficient response to the call to conversion. But she also promised the ultimate conversion of Russia, the triumph of her Immaculate Heart, at which point 'a certain period of grace will be granted to the world.' She showed the children a vision of hell, which underlined what's at stake in the Father's offer of mercy and pardon in His Son Jesus."[xxx]

Ralph Martin then summarizes the role of Mary. "These themes - imminent danger, the call to conversion and a promise of ultimate triumph - are characteristic of most of the apparitions of Mary throughout the century. A number of these have been judged worthy of belief by the local bishop after a time of investigation. Others are still under investigation. Some have been investigated and found wanting."[xxxi]

A Key to Understanding the Different Emphases

Both Our Lady and Pope John Paul II are trying to help prepare us for an encounter with the Lord in judgement and great mercy. Both are very much like John the Baptist trying to prepare the people for the first coming of Jesus Christ.

In Luke 7:29-35 the evangelist writes: "What comparison can I use for the men of today? What are they like? They are like children squatting in the city squares and calling to their playmates, 'We piped you a tune but you did not dance, we sang you a dirge, but you did not wail.' I mean that John the Baptizer came neither eating bread nor drinking wine, and you say, 'He is mad!' The Son of Man came and he both ate and drank, and you say, 'Here is a glutton and a drunkard, a friend of tax collectors and sinners!' God's wisdom is vindicated by all who accept it."[xxxii]

Ralph Martin makes this comparison come alive. "Mary is singing a dirge, weeping for her children who are in danger of being swept away by the imminent chastisement and judgment, in danger of eternal death, of hell. Yet many refuse to have their hearts broken by her tears; many refuse to respond to the profound simplicity of her repeated calls to conversion."[xxxiii]

Again Ralph Martin quotes St. Luke 19:41-45: "Coming within sight of the city, he wept over it and said: 'If only you had known the path to peace this day; but you have completely lost it from view! Days will come upon you when your enemies encircle you with a rampart, hem you in and press you hard from every side. They will wipe you out, you and your children within your walls, and leave not a stone on a stone within you, because you failed to recognize the time of your visitation.'"[xxxiv]

"A visitation from God is a two-edged sword; peace, the fullness of God's blessings, for those who are prepared; destruction for those who have failed to heed the preparatory messengers."[xxxv]

In the time of Jesus those who were baptized by John the Baptist were prepared for the message of Jesus. "The Pharisees and the lawyers, on the other hand, by failing to receive his baptism defeated God's plan in their regard (Luke 7:29-30)"[xxxvi]

As Ralph Martin puts it: "A bath of conversion, of repentance, of docility to the Holy Spirit, of intense sacramental life, is being administer by the Pope and Mary, to prepare us for an encounter with God. If we do not prepare, we may not be ready."[xxxvii]

Ralph Martin, the author of this article, has been for years a prophetic voice in the Catholic Charismatic movement. I feel his summary will open the eyes of many to the importance not only of the words of Pope John Paul, but the warning of Our Lady herself.

Martin concludes: "I believe we are now in a time of visitation. God is visiting us in the ministry of Pope John Paul II, in the ministry of Mary, and in many other ways. The time of preparation is well advanced. According to the message of Pope John Paul and Mary, we are on the verge of a significant action of God, an action that will function as a two-edged sword, depending on our preparation and willingness to respond. And isn't it possible that the fullness of the new springtime will not come until we are first purified through judgment or chastisement, and awakened to the holiness of God?"[xxxviii]

"Mary is weeping for those in danger of missing the visitation and has unveiled a personal plan of preparation for what is coming that involves prayer, fasting, repentance and reconciliation, daily Eucharist, Rosary, conversion and faith.

The messages are complementary. They are two edges of one sword. It is urgent that we respond."[xxxix]

****

We were fortunate in our parish retreat to have the testimony of two spirit filled parishioners, Beverly Fisher and Deacon John Weber. Beverly is the pious type that God the Father seems to feel perfectly at home speaking to her.. She is a down to earth, southern woman prayerful and cheerful. Beverly reminds me of the gifts of the Holy Spirit especially "joy, peace and patience."

For nearly 10 years I have been privileged to belong to a Teams of Our Lady group that includes Beverly and her husband Jim as well as Ronnie and Veralyn Alpha, Mike and Judy Campbell, Paul and Elli Borgatti, and Lou and Toni Hernandez. We are often amazed that God the Father shares things with Beverly that he wouldn't think of telling us men. Of course we men complain at our monthly dinner that Beverly gets most of the " visions".

A very interesting thing happened early on in the teams sharing. After dinner each participant had to share how God was working in their lives. Most of us had not yet been accustomed to the intimacy Beverly shared with God the Father. Beverly was telling us about one of her "visions", when Mike, a chemist, leaned over and said to Lou, "This is bull."

Then to Mike's own amazement, he shouted out, "no I don't believe it!"

"What is it Mike?" We asked.

"I see Jesus standing behind Fr. Carroll," the dumbfounded scientist revealed.

This group of close friends has been a source of joy and encouragement to me. I praised God the Father for His gifts to my children. Even though I have no great gifts, I encourage my parishioners to be totally open to the Holy

Spirit. After all, I remind them, I just take credit for their accomplishments as any good father does with his children.

****

Beverly Fisher

How did the Holy Spirit help me make Jesus Lord of my life? Such a simple question, now how do I explain nine years of experiences? It's impossible! All I can do is relate to you some of the circumstances that the Lord has walked me through, since my new encounter with the Holy Spirit.

Before I begin I think you should know just a few facts about my spirituality prior to my new awareness of God's presence in my life. I'm a cradle Catholic. I was born, baptized and raised Catholic. I went to Catholic school, married in the Catholic Church. Jim, my husband, and I attended Mass on Sundays, had our children baptized and educated in Catholic schools. It doesn't sound so bad, except there was something missing and I didn't even know it. In fact, I thought we were good Catholics and we were, at least in appearance.

As I collected my thoughts for this talk, I reflected back to the start of this new relationship with the Holy Spirit, which began in 1990. I can remember how after Sunday Mass, this same re-occuring question kept popping into my mind. "Why is it I only think about God for one hour on Sunday and not any other time of the week?"

After receiving communion one Sunday, I found myself telling God, "I know I haven't been as close to you as I should have been but there just doesn't seem to be enough hours in the day to do everything and find time for praying too. If you will just let me get the kids raised and out of the house, I'll try to be better and work more for your church." Exactly three days after our youngest child left for college,

God decided to collect on the promise I had made him. I found myself, along with my aunt and my dad at a family friend's house. She was Catholic and we heard she laid hands and prayed over people, she was "charismatic". We went for prayers for dad and the friend, Sharon Lowe, ended up praying for all of us. From that encounter, I knew something special had happened, as she prayed for me, tears were running down my checks. What I didn't realize at the time was that way down deep in me the long forgotten spark of the Holy Spirit was being re-kindled. Even though I received the Holy Spirit in baptism and confirmation, I had ignored him for a long time, almost forgetting about him.

That same afternoon, after being prayed over, I found myself kneeling in our family den wanting to pray but not sure how to or where to start. I remembered my friend had said she always went first to Our Lady and asked her intercession to Jesus. And so I prayed with my hands clasped together, "Mary, please hold my hand and take me closer to your Son, Jesus", at that moment I felt that my left hand had changed, it was like it wasn't my hand anymore but it was the softest skin I had ever felt and the fingers were so slender and delicate. Again the tears poured from my eyes. I knew I had felt the touch of Our Lady. From that moment on, I hungered and thirsted for all I could read, listen to or participate in, that related in any way to Jesus and Mary. I started reading the bible, going to daily Mass and was praying the rosary again. For the first 2 1/2 years of praying the rosary, especially the sorrowful mysteries, I cried and repented for my sins, not realizing God was healing me at the same time.

Within a year, Jim and I did the St. Louis deMontfort consecration to Jesus through Mary. We had our house enthroned to the Sacred Heart and later the Divine Mercy. I must admit, I did not understand fully what this meant as we consecrated our lives, our children, our home and possessions, but I would later find out. So I would have to say, the first steps for me in making Jesus Lord of my life, was to acknowledge there was a void, to be open to receive and then to ask mother Mary to bring me closer to her son, Jesus.

The next several years were wonderful, filled with so many beautiful prayer experiences and falling more and more in love with Jesus and his mother. After several years of retreats, conferences, seminars and days of recollection, I kept hearing various speakers talking about "embracing the cross." Finally in chapel, I asked the Lord to please explain what this meant. I believe that question changed the course of how I would handle the next four years. If I may make a suggestion at this point, you might want to consider starting with a simple question to Jesus and then build up to the big ones.

Starting in May 1995, our house was flooded as so many others in the area. Yes it was a shock to see 18 inches of water in your house, but in the midst of it all we had many beautiful friends who shared how much they cared and volunteered in the clean up, and through all the hard work we managed to share some fun experiences. And in the end God gave us a new home.

In March of '96, ten months after the flood, I went for a check up and they discovered I had a cancerous tumor on my kidney. They removed my right kidney and every thing was in my favor. It was a slow growing cancer and still contained. Now this is when I started to understand more of what the St. Louis deMontfort consecration meant. The week before learning of my cancer, God was so merciful to me. I was on retreat at a monastery in Ga. with my rosary group of ladies. During the days there, he was preparing me to climb the mountain as the character "much-afraid" did in the book *Hinds Feet on High Places*. This book was speaking so powerfully to me, I could only get through the first half, which ended with Psalm 91. Most of my friends know this is the special psalm I felt God gave to me to help me through the next weeks. The psalm is about the security of being under God's protection.

As I sat in the doctor's office that day, not knowing what he was about to tell me I was reading my St. Louis deMontfort consecration (day 23) page 53. "This devotion, consists then, in giving ourselves entirely to Our Lady, in order to belong entirely to Jesus Christ, through her. We must give to her: our body, with all its senses and members." Little did I know that in just a few minutes I would understand these words in the fullest sense. As I heard the words of the doctor describing what they had found and suspected, there was a small voice inside me that simply said, "yes". This little three-letter word somehow caused me to be at peace. I knew whatever the future was, it was out of my hands. What else could I do but go to Jesus through Mary. Because of this grace of acceptance, and trust I was as surprised as anyone at my reaction, even the doctor asked me if I understood what he was saying because most people get upset and some even angry and I seemed so calm. God continued to shower me with his mercy by giving me little gifts from heaven reaffirming that he was in control and with me at every step. I was under his protection. Oh, they were just little things, but they meant so much to me. I found out my doctor's last name Deus meant god. So I had Dr. God for my physician. The same day of the news I went to a healing Mass and the priest, Fr. Quinn, whom I had never met before, let me stand by him as he said Mass, and as he elevated the paten he told me to place myself there and give it all to Jesus, he said the congregation prayed for me and as I left he handed me a beautiful red rose. Through my devotion to St. Therese of the little flower I felt a rose had been sent from heaven for me that night. Two nights before my surgery, we met with our teams group and they offered the rosary for me and the room filled with the scent of roses. For some it was the first time they had experienced this heavenly scent. My surgery was scheduled for March 18, in between the feast of St. Patrick and St. Joseph. I can't think of a better pair to be sandwiched between. So you see I was truly under God's protection so what was there to fear.

A little over 2 months later, on June 4,1996, my father died of a heart attack. I couldn't believe this was happening so soon. Again God let me know he was in control and he let me know it in black and white. As dad was lying in intensive care, I was driving to the hospital to be with the family, and I passed a billboard on the side of the highway, which said in big bold letters: "read it, know it and believe it! Psalm 91." I went in to see dad, though he was unconscious, I bent down close to his ear and read the whole psalm to him. I don't know if it was more for him or me, but it is a moment that I'll never forget. A couple of weeks before dad died, he told me one night when I was visiting, that in his prayer time, usually after mom went to bed, he heard God say to him in answer to his prayers, "I'm all you'll ever need." That was the only time in dad's life he had ever experienced such a thing. I didn't recognize at the time but God was preparing daddy to come home.

Ten months after daddy died, on March 3,1997 my sister Deborah committed suicide. There are no words to explain the trauma of this situation. But again God in his mercy prepared me that night, for what was to happen. I had gone to 7:00 pm Sunday Mass and was in the middle of my adoration hour when Jim came into the chapel and told me the news. When I first heard the news I couldn't believe it, my body was shaking. On the inside, I wanted to run away from what had to be faced when I arrived at my mother's house where the family had gathered. Through the Mass, communion and adoration God was strengthening me in a supernatural way to get through this because in my natural human weakness, I wanted to run.

In prayer a few days afterwards I asked God to please let me know that Deborah was not alone in those last moments and that he was there with her. As I prayed, in my mind's eye the Lord let me see how Mary knelt down beside Deborah and took Deborah's soul and presented it to Jesus, who was standing there in the room with them. That brought me great relief to know she was not alone. A short time later I went into Deborah's bedroom where the accident happened and as I looked at the picture on the wall, I could not believe my eyes. There was this old picture of the Sacred Heart of Jesus and his hand was pointing to his heart. I was shocked I had never seen it before. In the picture, Jesus was looking in the direction of where Deborah had died. I could only take it as a gift from God to confirm my previous prayer experience. Shortly after that it was placed on my heart to receive my communions for Deborah. I've heard on Christmas and feasts days of our Lady that many souls are released from purgatory. To me purgatory is not a punishment but a place of cleansing life's debris to make us presentable to stand in front of the lord. On August 15th, Our Lady's Feast of the Assumption, I felt as if Jesus welcomed Deborah home.

After that I began to think how everything comes in threes. And perhaps this was the last of the events. I was wrong. On April 29, 1998, the doctor was suspicious of cancer and I had another surgery. Praise God it was not cancer. Again God's mercy intervened.

In April of 1999, the doctor's found another cancer. This time it was in my breast and there were two kinds, one more aggressive than the other. Exactly one year to the day from my last surgery, on April 29, the feast of St. Catherine of Siena, I had a lumpectomy and removal of the lymph nodes. It was detected early and had not spread. The prognosis is good and I will have started chemotherapy and radiation treatments. Again God was so merciful. The Friday night before I was to go for the biopsy the only scripture given at intercessory prayer was Psalm 91:14-16 "because he clings to me, I will deliver him; I will set him on high because he acknowledges my name. He shall call upon me, and I will answer him; I will be with him in distress; I will deliver him and glorify him; with length of days I will gratify him and will show him my salvation." The day before the biopsy I received a gift from a priest, it was a key chain and inscribed on the back was a verse, "do not fear, the Lord is with you every step of the way." You see how good my God is, sometimes he puts things in writing for me.

After reflecting back on these events, I realize it all began with a question of acknowledging there was a void in my life. "I wonder why I only think of God for one hour on Sunday?"

Yes there have been some difficult times, some tears, fears and anxieties but because of God's mercy, he has given me new eyes to see not just the circumstances around me but his presence in each and every one of them. Through the enrichment of the sacraments God has made it easier for me to hear with the ears of my heart and to see through the eyes of my soul. Without these new eyes, I could have missed all the road signs he left for me along this road we have walked the past nine years. I know that each day as I give my little "yes" and accept whatever cross he gives me, if I offer it up to him he will give back to me the grace to embrace the cross and my burden becomes lighter. I know God's not through with me and I don't know what lies ahead but I have a God who wants to walk every step of the way with me. And all I had to do was acknowledge, accept, and ask Our Lady.

I would like to conclude with this short story about a teacup. It's such a simple little story line but has a powerful message.

There was a couple who used to go to England to shop in the beautiful stores. They both liked antiques and pottery and especially teacups. This was their twenty-fifth wedding anniversary. One day in this shop they saw a beautiful teacup. They said, "may we see that?"

As the lady handed it to them, the teacup suddenly spoke. You don't understand," It said. "I haven't always been a teacup. There was a time when I was red and I was clay. My master took me and rolled me and patted me over and over and I yelled out, 'let me alone', but he only smiled, not yet."

Then he put me in the oven. I never felt such heat. I wondered why he wanted to burn me and I yelled and knocked at the door. I could see him through the opening and I could read his lips as he shook his head, 'not yet'.

Finally the door opened, he put me on the shelf, and I began to cool. "There that's better," I said. And he brushed and painted me all over.

The fumes were horrible. I thought I would gag. "Stop it, stop it!" I cried. He only nodded, "Not yet."

Then suddenly he put me bank into the oven, not like the first one. This was twice as hot and I knew I would suffocate. I begged. I pleaded. I screamed. I cried. All the time I could see him through the opening nodding his head saying, "Not yet."

I knew there wasn't any hope. I would never make it. I was ready to give up. But the door opened and he took me out and placed me on the shelf. One hour later he handed me a mirror and said, "Look at yourself," and I did. I said "That's not me; that couldn't be me. It's beautiful. I'm beautiful."

"I want you to remember, then," he said, "I know it hurts to be rolled and patted, but if I had left you alone, you'd have dried up. I know it made you dizzy to spin around on the wheel, but if I had stopped, you would have crumbled. I know it hurt and was hot and disagreeable in the oven, but if I hadn't put you there, you would have cracked. I know the fumes were bad when I brushed and painted you all over, but if I hadn't done that, you never would have hardened; You would not have any color in your life. And if I hadn't put you back in the second oven, you wouldn't survive for very long because the hardness would not have held. Now you are a finished product. You are what I had in mind when I first began you."

MORAL:

God knows what He's doing ,for all of us. He is the Potter, and we are his clay. He will mold us and make us, so that we may be made into flawless pieces of work to fulfill His good, pleasing, and perfect will. And He is always watching over us.

Don't try to hold God's hand; let Him hold yours. Let Him do the holding and you the trusting.

Hammer William Webb-Peploe

****

Author's Note: Deacon Weber has been involved in the charismatic movement for many years. John has had an amazing rapport with the Holy Spirit. He brings a down to earth, Texas approach to religion. John is able to put everyone at ease.

What touches most of our parishioners are his homilies. Deacon Weber has one of the most unique gifts of the Holy Spirit, the gift of tears. It is rather extraordinary to see this scientist weeping like a little boy when he delivers a sermon. Our Blessed Mother really loves little children...even little boys.

Although John has been active for years in our convert program (R.C.I.A.), and worked hard to become an expert in the annulment process in order to validate marriages in the Catholic Church, his greatest strength in the Holy Spirit is his greatest weakness. More men, particularly fathers could learn from Deacon Weber. Real men...real fathers know how to cry. It's a gift of the Holy Spirit

****

Deacon Johnny Weber
From Deer Hunter to Deacon

Since I am still a deer hunter, the title "From Deer Hunter to Deacon" probably is a misleading title. As I speak, you can reflect on what I say and maybe decide on a more appropriate title.

How we see ourselves, how we judge ourselves can influence our lives either good or bad. Knowing about God is one thing; to experience God on a personal level – to be able to say "Wow, I have been touched by God" can also influence our lives either good or bad.

I will begin my story as a teenager, because that is a time in life when we can be very sensitive about how we see ourselves. I saw myself as a skinny, ugly, not very exciting person. I did little dating. In the late 50's athletic ability was a prized asset. I had no athletic ability. In high school, I learned that I had the skills necessary to be a good duck hunter. I would get up as early as I needed to, walk as far as I needed to, crawl in the mud if necessary to get my limit of ducks. If those hunting with me had difficulty getting their ducks, no problem – I would get part of their limit too. At this time in my life, I went to church but was not close to God. I was sure that God had no interest in my life – didn't even know who I was. God would judge me, however, upon my death.

In 1960, the year before Jaynell and I were married, I made my first deer hunt. In a few years, I learned that I was as good a deer hunter as I was a duck hunter. I can remember how proud I felt when one of my sisters told me that two of my older brothers-in-law were envious of my

88

deer hunting success. When we moved to Slidell in 1972, I was able to add squirrel and turkey hunting to my quest. I put a lot of energy and time into these hunting endeavors.

My relationship with God was no different than in high school. God didn't know whom I was – I was to make sure that I didn't die with a mortal sin on my soul. Jaynell and I had a good marriage, but we were not real close. I wanted her to have other interest – to spend times doing things with other people so I would be free "to do my thing". I could not wait until my son could be a hunter like his dad. I even took my daughter duck hunting but she had to wash her gloves the night before – clean gloves for a duck hunt. Some of our vacations were to check out new hunting opportunities. You may have heard me mention an industrial psychologist named Morris Massey. He says that we are creatures of habit and our behavior does not change unless we have a significant emotional event. A significant emotional event is not necessarily a crying event, but an event that affects more than our head – affects something inside (our heart, our soul, our inner being).

Marriage Encounter – A Significant Event

In 1974, Jaynell and I went on a Marriage Encounter Weekend. Jaynell understood what the Sacrament of Matrimony could be and should be, and she wanted it for us. I could see the conflict right away. She told me of the hurt and loneliness my hunting activities caused her. She told me how it felt to know that she was not #1 in my life. In 1975, Jaynell and I went on a weekend to prepare us to give Marriage Encounter weekends as a team couple. On Saturday afternoon of the weekend, the team priest, Fr. Chuck Gallagher asked each couple to share – facing the 34 couples and 7 priests on the question "What do I know I have to change to be a better husband or a better wife?" I started shaking and crying immediately; as we shared I tried to explain my emotion. I said John Weber equals Hunter. If I give it up, what will I be? I will lose my identity. The next day Fr. Gallagher told each couple and priest goodbye, one at a time. He looked into my eyes, from a very short distance and said, "I'm sorry about the hunting but you are now a fisher of men." At that moment I did not see Fr. Gallagher as Fr. Gallagher, it was like Jesus himself was speaking to me. At that moment it was like I was on the shore of the Sea of Galilee and Jesus Himself was calling me to be a fisher-of-men. I had a significant emotional event.

A few years later finds me still struggling to be a big time hunter and live the Sacrament of Matrimony. We went to a Catholic Charismatic Conference and heard a sermon by a Redemptorist priest, Fr. Tom Forrest. He made a statement "Whatever we think about the most during the day is our God".

A few years after that, I overheard someone listening to an audiotape by Fr. John Bertolucci. He was speaking on Isaiah 43:1 "Fear not, for I have redeemed you; I have called you by name: you are mine." He said no matter where we are spiritually, there is more. I kept reflecting on that reading. What a revelation for me, the God who created the universe knows me by name. He says "John you are mine." God was and is telling me that my life wasn't just for me. I was not put on this earth for the purpose of enjoying hunting and fishing. The God who knows me by name was and is telling me that my priorities in life are loving my wife, children, grandchildren and others. Hunting is only recreation, not a purpose for living.

It was so hard for me to put hunting in its proper priority. I tried to blame others for my dilemma. Jaynell just needed to understand me. Of course, I used the old standard rationale, "I don't hang around bars, don't chase women, and you knew that I hunted when you married me. Now I can look back and see why hunting was such an obsession. Because of years and years of low self-esteem and then feeling good about my hunting skills – it became my identity.

He Knows Me By Name

After years of struggles I now see that dignity comes from being known by name. I have dignity because God cares about me and has plans for me. Most of the time I feel good about being John Weber. He knows me by name.

Each fall, as the weather cools, the old feelings and interests come back. I have two main reasons to resist making hunting the center of my life. One is knowing that God has other plans for me. Secondly, Jaynell keeps challenging me to keep my priorities in order and to live the Sacrament of Matrimony that we are called to by God.

I guess I better talk about being a deacon for a little bit. In the early 80's, I had this sense that I was being called to be a deacon. I didn't tell anyone because I wanted the idea to go away. It would not go away. At an ordination to the priesthood for Transitional Deacon, Johnny Planea, I got the message loud and clear – God wanted me to be a Deacon. I thought "Why don't you call someone else, there are probably a lot of people who would like to be a Deacon."

I finally told Jaynell and Fr. Carroll hoping they would not laugh. Archbishop Hannan ordained me after 3 ½ years of night school, on December 12, 1987. Being a Deacon has been very rewarding to me, especially in dealing with RCIA. Being a Deacon, however, has really messed up my turkey seasons, which are in the spring when I am really busy with RCIA. Oh well!

I truly enjoy the outdoors. It is a challenge for me to hunt, to outsmart deer, turkeys and squirrels. But I know that it must remain for me just a form of recreation – like fishing is for me. I can never allow hunting to again become my purpose for life. I have obligations to my wife, my family, my God and my church that must remain in the proper priority.

For a long time I saw myself as a hunter of Bambi, now I finally understand that I have a higher calling, to be a fisher-of-men.

****

Mike Campbell - as recounted by his wife Judy

Sometimes it seems that Our Blessed Mother and God want certain individuals to become friends to help each other on the spiritual journey to heaven. In January, 1990, such a group, "Teams of Our lady" was formed in Slidell.. "Teams of Our Lady" is an international movement to help families grow spiritually through the guidance of the Blessed Mother. Five or six couples and a priest meet once a month for a rosary, dinner, and an evening discussing our spiritual struggles and blessings.

September 5, 1992

We had our regular Team of Our Lady dinner at Dr. Luis & Toni Hernandez's home. As we sat talking, Mike was seated in a recliner in front of a corner bookcase in their den. Fr. Carroll was directly opposite Mike. Behind Father was a corner of the den with a crucifix on a wall surrounded by pictures of Katie Hernandez. Katie, four years old, died of leukemia February 19, 1992. Mike started crying again and said, "Excuse me for crying but I am seeing Fr. Carroll on the crucifix behind where he is sitting instead of Jesus." Mike was very upset by it for the rest of the night. He later told Judy that the odd thing was that Father was not dressed in his priestly garments but in clothing like he wore that night to our teams meeting.

Sunday, September 13, 1992

Mike, our skeptical chemist had another supernatural experience. We went to different Masses and when he walked in the house after 10:00 am Mass, he was very pale and looked sick to me. I asked, "What's wrong? Don't you feel well?" He told me this experience. When he received Communion, he went back to his pew to pray. With his eyes shut in prayer, he was above our church looking down and saw with three dimensional figures that our church was totally covered by a bubble or dome like Mike has seen used to house underwater divers. All around the bubble was blackness, but all those inside the church were protected. A voice twice said to Mike, "You will be saved! You will be saved!" At first his interpretation was protection from a tidal wave. However, after he heard me talk to Colleen Kelley and she said maybe it was protection against New Age or something, Mike said that it was protection against something bad, but he's not sure what.

October 16, 1993

We were at a Team's meeting Saturday night at the Hernandez's house when Mike saw something during the team rosary that precedes our dinner meeting.

Mike saw a vision similar to St. John Bosco's vision of a Pope guiding the church through troubled times. Mike saw Fr. Carroll holding the Eucharist at the front of the ship while several priests were rowing the boat. Serpents were leaping out of the water as the boat moved through the water.

Chapter 6
Eucharist

"No one can come to me unless the Father who sent me draws him; I will raise him up on the last day. ... I myself am the living bread come down from heaven. If anyone eats this bread he shall live forever; the bread I will give is my flesh, for the life of the world."(John 6:44, 51-52)

"The first announcement of the Eucharist divided the disciples, just as the announcement of the Passion scandalized them: 'This is a hard saying; who can listen to it?' The Eucharist and the Cross are stumbling blocks. It is the same mystery and it never ceases to be an occasion of division. 'Will you also go away?' (John 6:67) The Lord's question echoes through the ages, as a loving invitation to discover that only he has 'the words of eternal life.'(John 6:68) and that to receive in faith the gift of his Eucharist is to receive the Lord himself. "[xl]
(Catechism of the Catholic Church)

"But since Christ is the only way to the Father, in order to highlight his living and saving presence in the church and the world, the International Eucharistic Congress will take place in Rome, on the occasion of the Great Jubilee. The year 2000 will be intensely Eucharistic: in the Sacrament of the Eucharist the Savior, who took flesh in Mary's womb twenty centuries ago, continues to offer himself to humanity as the source of divine life. "[xli]
(Pope John Paul, II * Tertio-Millennio Adventiente)

Author's Note: Since December 1983 parishioners of St. Margaret Mary have had Perpetual Adoration of the Blessed Sacrament in our chapel. Twenty-four hours a day seven days a week for nearly sixteen years hundreds of Catholics have honored Jesus as Lord of our lives by spending time praying before the consecrated host which is contained in a monstrance.

The Theology of the Eucharist

The word Eucharist means to give thanks. It is based on a promise and its fulfillment. Jesus made us an extraordinary promise in St. John's gospel (6:51-56) Jesus said: "I myself am the living bread come down from heaven. If anyone eats this bread he shall live forever; ... He who feeds on my flesh and drinks my blood has eternal life ... The man who feeds on my flesh and drinks my blood remains in me, and I in him."

The context of this promise was the occasion of a great miracle. Jesus had just fed five thousand by multiplying loaves and fishes. Eight times he told his audience "he was the living bread" 4 times he insisted that they eat his flesh and drink his blood in order to have eternal life."

The Crowd Leaves

After experiencing this great miracle of the multiplication of loaves and fish we must be surprised at the reaction of the crowd. They said: "This sort of talk is hard to endure! How can anyone take it seriously?"(John 6:60) The vast majority of the witnesses left because of a lack of belief.

Jesus must have been discouraged. He then asks the Twelve, "Do you want to leave me too?" Peter responds: "Lord, to whom shall we go? You have the words of eternal life. We have come to believe; we are convinced that you are God's holy one."(John 6:67-68) I believe that Judas betrayed Jesus later not for the money, but because like so many Christians today he simply could not believe that Jesus could do what he promised...give himself to us in the Eucharist.

A Promise Fulfilled

At the Last Supper Jesus fulfilled his promise to the crowd, to the apostles and to each of us. It was at a passover meal that the Jews celebrate each deliverance from bondage, freedom from the Egyptians.

"Then, taking bread and giving thanks, he (Jesus) broke it and gave it to them, saying: 'This is my body to be given for you. Do this as a remembrance of me.' He did the same with the cup after eating, saying as he did so: 'This cup is the new covenant in my blood, which will be shed for you.'"(Luke 22:19-20)

Catholic Catechism

The new Catholic Catechism explains why we adore Jesus present in this bread and wine consecrated at Mass. "Because Christ himself is present in the sacrament of the altar, he is to be honored with the worship of adoration. 'To visit the Blessed Sacrament is ... a proof of gratitude, an expression of love, and a duty of adoration toward Christ our Lord."xlii

When Catholics are asked if they have a personal relationship with Christ they often cannot answer that question. But if you reflect upon that question you realize that you have a personal relationship with Christ through faith that comes in baptism. You also have a personal relationship with Jesus through your reception of Holy Communion. You receive his very body and blood, soul and divinity. You too can say with St. Paul, "... the life I live now is not my own; Christ is living in me."(Galatians 2:20)

History of Adoration at St. Margaret Mary

In December 1983, Fr. Martin Lucia preached at all of our Masses. I had agreed reluctantly to let him speak about Perpetual Adoration. I did not expect him to get 500 people to agree to spend one hour a week before the Blessed Sacrament in the chapel.

As a young priest at St. Francis of Assisi in New Orleans we tried to have adoration of the Blessed Sacrament on first Fridays only. "Sign up for one hour only I pleaded. This is just once a month. The hours are set from 7 am Friday to 6 am Saturday the next day."

For a short time it worked. But the early hours were too hard. We then stopped at midnight. Within five years adoration on first Fridays died out at St. Francis of Assisi. This was at a time, 1959-64, when 85% of Catholics went to church every Sunday.

Perhaps the success Fr. Lucia had was due to our patroness St. Margaret Mary. This visitation nun had been entrusted by Jesus himself with the task of spreading devotion to the Eucharist as a way of honoring the Sacred Heart of Jesus. First Friday devotion and adoration of Jesus were hallmarks of her ministry.

Perpetual Adoration - Shortcut to the Father

Fr. Lucia was a terrible speaker. He was short and thin. I really felt sorry for him. I thought they were going to run him out of town. I didn't realize the power of intercession of Saint Margaret Mary herself. God the Father wanted places of honor for His Son. Over 500 signed up on December 3, 1983. We have had adoration continuously now for nearly 16 years.

When St. Margaret Mary Parish was divided, St. Luke's Parish, was formed. Almost immediately Fr. Hall, the new pastor, initiated Perpetual Adoration. It has flourished there ever since. I am sure that at least 1,000 Catholics in Slidell, Louisiana are committed to adoration at least one hour a week.

Gallup poll claims only 37 % of American Catholics believe in the real presence of Jesus in the Eucharist. The numbers who attend weekly Mass regularly are now only about 25 %. Why? They simply do not believe the words of Jesus, and his promise of eternal life. "If you do not eat the flesh of the Son of Man and drink his blood, you have no life in you. He who feeds on my flesh and drinks my blood has life eternal and I will raise him up on the last day."(John 6:53-54)

Catholics who wonder if they are "saved" need to ask themselves only one question; do I really believe what Jesus said? Faith in the real presence is a sign not only that we are saved but also that we have a deep personal relationship with Jesus Christ.

In addition to the 1,000 that are "signed up" there are thousands who just drop in the chapel to speak to Jesus. Many non-Catholics who hunger for a personal relationship with Jesus find themselves drawn to the chapel for private prayer. Our community not only believes in the real presence of Jesus in communion, but we put that faith into practice in Perpetual Adoration.

How do I know that adoration of Jesus draws us to the heart of God the Father? Once when Jesus was speaking of God the Father, Philip one of the early apostles said to Jesus: "Lord, ... show us the Father and that will be enough of us."(John 14:8)

"'Philip,' Jesus replied, 'after I have been with you all this time, you still do not know me? Whoever has seen me has seen the Father.'"(John 14:8-9) Adoration of the Blessed Sacrament is a shortcut to the heart of God the Father.

****

There are two important elements for the success of Perpetual Adoration: example and organization. Bernie

McClelland is the organizer. Fr Mossy Gallagher gives us the example of daily adoration.

Bernie has been in charge of the day to day operations for a number of years. If someone is unable to fulfill his or her hour commitment, Bernie will call a substitute. She frequently fills in for someone who is unable to make his or her hour of adoration

****

Bernie McClelland
Eucharistic Adoration

Fr. Martin Lucia, SS. CC., was invited to our parish to give a talk on Perpetual Adoration, a ministry he was promoting all over the nation, if we could but follow the message. And we did on December 1983. At that time Father presented a working formula that would assure the proper management of our ministry, which we knew little about.

After Father Lucia made his presentation at one of the Masses, I happened to meet with him in the sacristy, at which time he told me he needed a car to drive to churches in Mississippi and Alabama to bring his message as he had been called to do. Since I was the only one present at the time, I presumed he was asking me for my car.

Now, Father had no idea what kind of car I had – it could have been a jalopy. It so happened I had a spanking new Oldsmobile which was the pride and joy of my life. That car was a gift from God (with payments of course) but I also placed it next to God. I was so overwhelmed with his request I was speechless. I told him I would have to check my work schedule to see if I could be without a car for a few days before I said yes.

God was already at work on this project. My schedule for the days he needed the car just happened to correspond very well. I was beginning to bend a little and finally I called my insurance agent to check out the state coverage and some other details before I agreed. Everything fell into place and so I filled the gas tank and brought the car to him. After he left I had no qualms about the deal, only a recurring thought – why did I do that? Remember, I wasn't part of perpetual adoration yet.

On that weekend announcements were made to solicit workers, telephone people, coordinators, prayers, etc. Since I thought I was a wizard at telephone contacts, I signed up for the lowest job possible knowing I could do very well with it. And I did. I now had one foot in the water. God was working.

Feeling very comfortable with my new job, I decided to give adoration a try. So I signed up for an hour, Wednesday at 7:00 pm. My only experience with adoration at that time was the 40 hours devotion I participated in at grade school level. I attended Sacred Heart school throughout grade and high school and knew very little about adoration. We had novena devotions and benediction every Friday but no adoration for students. I began to realize I didn't know how to pray. I said my rosary and asked God to grant favors to different loved ones or friends. It never crossed my mind to ask for the grace of prayer. Instead I collected some booklets on adoration to help me along.

For a short while things stood as they were. I was making my phone calls and making my hour when on a Sunday morning while trying to beat the celebrant up the aisle, one of the coordinators came up behind me and said, "I'm bringing my papers to you. I'm moving this weekend." When I turned to say "No", she had crossed over the aisle and seated herself where I couldn't get to her.

The words stayed with me, but I didn't worry. I knew I could give them to someone else.

On that afternoon I became ill and had to crash on the couch. In other words I was grounded with aches and a fever of 102. I gave little thought to the lady who was leaving town. About 10:30 pm the phone rang and again the lady said she was coming right over. I told her I was ill and in bed for the night. I suggested she leave the papers on the table in the chapel so that I could pick them up and give them to the proper person. When I got to chapel several days later, there were no papers. I soon began to realize I was the coordinator for 6:00 pm – 12 Midnight adoration. God was indeed working.

Soon I found myself filling in for several difficult times and I recall sharing with my daughter when I had to go for the third time in one week – "I'm just not this holy! I wasn't wholly convinced that I was being called to be there.

In order to help the ministry along I prepared most of the paper work, keeping the books, watching for vacancies, etc. with the main coordinator, the late Margaret Mary Bobeck, no coincidence but planned by God. She was the person who lovingly gave her time to every phase of the ministry, while I, the Martha, was looking for the earthly approach. I became more willing and less reluctant, though God was winning!

Soon I began to look forward to my hours in adoration and finally I began thanking God for the privilege of being his friend and companion.

It is a well-known fact that I am a Martha except God has made it possible by grace to let me share Mary's love for Jesus in the Blessed Sacrament as she did in Galilee.

I yearned to be in His presence, to tell Him about my day, my needs, the decisions I had to make, the things I was looking forward to. Even away from His presence I now know if I call on Him before taking on a task, I do not walk alone. It is only when I take over that things go wrong. I kiddingly told a friend, a casual believer, one day "I think Jesus is in my back pocket." I feel the presence of his angels when I am in chapel during the night or working in the church alone.

I have received so many beautiful scriptures while in prayer for myself and the ministries I serve. One day while very burdened about a health problem I received Matthew 6, "therefore I tell you do not worry about your life, what you will eat, drink or about your body or what you will wear. Can anyone by worrying add a single moment to his life? Seek ye first the kingdom of God and all else will be given to you. Do not worry about tomorrow, tomorrow will take care of itself." I try to live totally dependent on God.

On one particular evening as I prayed, flames began to surround the corpus on the crucifix above the altar. Almost simultaneously they surrounded the Sacred Host in the monstrance. I received words "My sacrifice on the cross is the same as the one on the altar. My mercy is everlasting to sinners."

And long before that, Isaiah 45: "I will go before and level the mountains; bronze doors I will shatter and iron bars I will snap. I will give you treasures out of the darkness and riches that have been hidden away that you may know I am the Lord, the God of Israel who calls you by name." How could I answer? I was speechless. My God is an awesome God.

Some of the faithful have reported incredible stories directly related with their adoration and worship. One man who had a weekly hour from 6:00 – 7:00 am was awakened by his alarm clock at 5:30 am. As he left his bedroom he noticed a slight haze around his ceiling. He again thought he saw a haze as he crossed the den going to the garage door. As he opened that door the alarm went off. Flames were climbing the inside wall into the attic through the attic fan. He was able to call the fire department and fortunately all members of the family were evacuated before the house was completely demolished. He knows that if he hadn't gotten up as he did at 5:30 am for adoration they more than likely would not have survived. You see the other days they did not get up until 7:00 am.

Another a young woman battling death from cancer for months, suffered so much, especially at night, that on one night when things were unbearable she had her mother put her in the car and bring her to the chapel. There she lay prostrate on the floor before the Blessed Sacrament for as long as she could tolerate the pain. She left with the peace that only a loving Lord could grace her with and an acceptance of her inevitable death which came not long afterward. Her courage became known to all and her joyful union with God glorified Him in the highest.

A gentleman reported that the difficulties in his marriage were so great, he was contemplating divorce. One night back in 1987, after a horrible argument with his wife, he left the house with the idea of going to a bar to find a female companion to soothe his misery. When he got to a traffic light, it turned red and suddenly he had a thought to go to the chapel, with which he was not too familiar. He disregarded the thought and decided he would go to the bar as he had planned. The inner voice again said, "go to the chapel". The struggle continued; bar, chapel, bar, chapel. The light turned green and he went to the chapel. The chapel only had a couple of people in it and on the bench there was an open bible, which he read for about two hours. He felt the love and the peace of God for which he longed. He also renewed a commitment to save his marriage and now spends at least an hour weekly in adoration, sharing with Jesus his sad and good times, laughing and crying with Him. He knows he has been transformed through the love of Jesus and the Eucharistic Presence in the chapel. Our God is so real to us!

A devout Eucharistic Minister has related how she sees the suffering face of Christ and sometimes the sorrowful Mother Mary in the Eucharist as she prays before the Blessed Sacrament when preparing to bring Holy Communion to the sick and dying. She carries these images in her heart and her memory while making her rounds, extending His mercy and compassion to each one as she ministers to them.

Then there was the lady who dropped into the chapel one Saturday morning to pray about her 16-year old daughter and what had transpired with her the night before. She cried and rambled on for a while when suddenly she felt very calm and expressed that to Jesus. She told him that she shouldn't feel so good because nothing had changed except for the way she felt – as though someone had put an arm around her and assured her that everything was going to be okay. She began to hear a choir practicing in the church. It was barely audible – she couldn't make out the words but the music was beautiful. As she relaxed and listened the thought came how lucky we were to have such a beautiful choir. When she left the chapel shortly after, she decided she wanted to get closer to the choir to hear the beautiful singing. As she entered the vestibule from the chapel she could see that the church was empty and in darkness. Realizing she had experienced a special gift from God, she returned to the chapel to thank Jesus and his Holy Mother for allowing her to hear the angels sing. These are just a few of the graces given to those who spend time in adoration of the Blessed Sacrament.

Many, many petitions have been granted to those who fervently pray in faith time and time again. Lives have been changed, jobs sought and found, children have reconciled with their parents and seemingly impossible prayers have been answered all through the mercy of God through his loving Son present on our altar.

We pray dear Lord that being ever mindful of your presence in the Blessed Sacrament, we will turn to you in all of our needs and sorrows, gratefully acknowledging your gifts to us by praising and glorifying God for all eternity.

****

Author's Note: Fr. Mossy Gallagher, an associate pastor since 1978, is a tremendous example to all of us. Fr. Gallagher spends an hour in adoration each and every day.

It is a source of inspiration for all of us to see this dedicated priest praying in the chapel. He is a powerhouse of prayer for the sick and elderly. Although his primary work at St. Margaret Mary has been a ministry to the sick, the prayer component makes his ministry effective.

The late Bishop Fulton Sheen recommended a daily hour of adoration to priests in every clergy retreat he preached. Bishop Sheen himself kept that commitment his entire life. Fr. Gallagher has had that same kind of impact at St. Margaret Mary since his arrival. This prayerful priest is a joy to our community.

In April 1999, Fr. Mossy Gallagher celebrated 50 years of priesthood. We pray that God the Father will keep him with us for many more years. He is the inspiration we all need.

****

Fr. Mossy Gallagher
An Hour A Day of Adoration

"Could you not watch one hour with me?"(Matthew 26:40) That is the challenge that most people respond to when they become involved in Eucharistic Devotion; the challenge that comes to us usually from perhaps a casual reading of John's Gospel. For me, as I recently reflected back 50 years of priesthood, it seems to me now that I was awakened to that call in my early boyhood years.

Our home was situated next to the Parish church of St. Joseph. I can remember coming home after a visit to Granny's or to the local grocery store. As we passed the darkened church, lighted only by the small but vigorous flame of the sanctuary lamp, we went in for a visit if the door was still open. Invariably, open or shut, my mother did her evangelizing, gently reminding me that Jesus was lonely if the church was empty and how glad He was to see us and gave His full attention to our whispered prayer.

Later on I wrestled with the choice of becoming a priest and serve God's people in my home diocese or on far-flung mission fields. The "lonely" Jesus won that decision too. I am sure there were other determining factors that may have had an influence on my decision, but adoration of the Blessed Sacrament was certainly one of the most important.

Often times I felt like the keeper of the lighthouse far out to sea and I would feel Jesus using me to all the weary travelers, to break the journey, rest a while and visit the Good Shepherd and regain lost energy and focus.

That is precisely what he is calling many or most of us to tonight. Remember this invitation is meant for all – "Come to me all you who are weary and find life burdensome, I will refresh you!"(Matthew 11:28)

Respond to this call – He does not renege, fall down on His promises. "Jesus come to me – reveal yourself to me – let me see the beauty of your face." Your church gives us 4 pictures of you:

A.   That painted by St. Matthew, "The Jewish Jesus
B.   The picture by St Mark-similar but different
C.   The picture painted by St Luke-the gentile gospel
D.   The picture painted by St John-the one who Loved Jesus enough to stand under the cross.

My favorite prayer in adoration is to picture Jesus, as seen in the gospels. You too can get a glimpse of your own picture of Jesus, I would suggest you try St. Luke. St. Luke, like ourselves, is non-Jewish and perhaps that is the perspective we can get most out of in prayer. Luke certainly has the Gospel of the common man.

Remember always in your exercise of trying to get to know Jesus better and to love Him more faithfully, there are several helps we can use. For instance, St. Ignatius tells us to use all our faculties to visualize Jesus and as the picture becomes "Clearer on our Screen" the heart will also love at a quicker pace. Nobody can get close to Jesus, see the Beauty of His Countenance, and not be moved to love Him more faithfully.

I find it useful to look forward to my time before the Eucharist. I compare it to a person who is terminally ill and has come for radiation treatment. Jesus' healing love radiates from the Eucharist and even if you have come and many times have fallen asleep at the exercise, the Divine Physician will remind you as He reminds me so many times that He is the healer, nobody or nothing else. Try to picture the eyes of Jesus and as you do so begin to feel the power of his gaze upon you. You may not be receiving the healing that you were looking for but perhaps there is a deeper healing that is being given to you that you are completely unconscious of that you need far more. Many of us, as we visit the chapel, are tired and weary of the struggles of the workplace and our daily chores. Remind Jesus of His beautiful invitation to come to Him yes weary and tired and sleepy as we are. All we have to do is be faithful, spend that hour, and don't earn the rebuke of "Could you not watch one hour with me?" What does He want you for? That is no business of yours or mine to inquire. All we are called upon to do is to be faithful. The good servant is always standing by his or her master when called and stays until he or she is dismissed. That is what fidelity means. That is what discipleship means. Just be faithful.

****

Judy Campbell

Authors Note: Judy Campbell is a convert to the Catholic faith. She is currently teaching religion at St Margaret Mary School.

I developed a strong hunger for learning all I could about Holy Communion and received it as often as possible. I read three books over a few months that greatly influenced me. The books were *Eucharistic Miracle* by Joan Cruz, *Miracles Do Happen* by Sister Briege McKenna, and *This is My Body, This is My Blood: Miracles of the Eucharist* by Bob and Penny Lord. If I sat close enough to the front during Mass, paid great attention to the Mass, constantly thanked God and Mary for being allowed to learn how precious Mass and Communion are, and watched carefully, the large Communion Host that the priest holds up had a gold edge like the gold leaf on a Bible. I was real curious if the priest consumed that Communion Host that he always laid on the altar or if this gold edged Host was just a visual aid to remind us on how special and more precious than gold Mass is for all of us. After seeing it several times, I asked Mike, my husband if the one that is gold edged is the same one that the priest consumes. Mike was an altar boy for several years and I figured he would know. He said the Host is not gold edged and I must be seeing things. To be honest, I had never paid that much attention to the consecration before or sat up front during Mass. I continued to watch and sometimes saw that both pieces were also gold edged that the priest consumes.

December 15, 1987
I had the most wonderful experience of my life in the chapel at St. Margaret Mary Church. I had attended Mass, stayed for the rosary, and then stayed to pray the St. Bridget prayers in the Pieta book. I had started praying them October 15, 1987. As I finished and was ready to leave, I felt an inner urging, not a voice but a message in my mind, inviting me to come closer. I picked up my things and moved to the front row of the chapel, as close as I could get to the Blessed Sacrament. For the next few minutes (fifteen minutes to a half-hour), I just sat there not praying, not thinking, not doing anything but soaking up the most wonderful love I have ever felt in my entire life. It was the most wonderful, indescribable feeling I have ever had.

I know that in spite of loving parents, sisters, friends, husband, and three sons, no one has ever showered me with so much love before. I wish I had words to describe the experience. Books on near death experiences describe similar frustration at describing the love that comes from Jesus. I felt like I never wanted to leave the chapel. Even though I know I have always loved God my whole life, this love was extremely lopsided. God loved me so much more than I was capable of loving him in return. The closest way to describe the experience is to compare it to one of those rare moments when my boys were infants. The best experience with them was after the house was quiet; I was all alone with the baby; nursing him, holding him, giving him my total love and undivided attention. The baby is incapable of returning the love at that point in his life and the Mother knows it, but loves him deeply. I felt like I was the infant and God was the Mother that morning in the chapel. I will never fear anything except displeasing God and losing the chance to experience that love again in heaven some day. Eventually I had the feeling that I had a busy day ahead of me and Jesus reluctantly felt that I had better leave. The overwhelming intensity of the love gradually decreased or I could never have torn myself away from the chapel.

Chapter 7
Healing

"The Beatitudes respond to the natural desire for happiness. This desire is of divine origin: God has placed it in the human heart in order to draw man to the One who alone can fulfill it: We all want to live happily; in the whole human race there is no one who does not assent to this proposition, even before it is fully articulated. ... God alone satisfies. "[xliii]

(Catechism of the Catholic Church)

"The Beatitudes are at the heart of Jesus' preaching. ... The Beatitudes fulfill the promises by ordering them no longer merely to the possession of a territory, but to the Kingdom of heaven: ... Blessed are those who are persecuted for righteousness' sake, for theirs is the kingdom of heaven. "[xliv]

(Catechism of the Catholic Church)

"At the end of the second millennium, the church has once again become a Church of martyrs. The persecutions of believers - priests, religious and laity - has caused a great sowing of martyrdom in different parts of the world. The witness of Christ borne even to the shedding of blood has become a common inheritance of Catholics, Orthodox, Anglicans and Protestants, ... "[xlv]

*(Pope John Paul, II * Tertio Millennio Adventiente)*

Author's Note: There was a great disappointment I am sure that Mother Nadine Brown would note be able to participate in our parish retreat. I did not learn of her decision until I returned from Fatima in the middle of May. The retreat was scheduled for June 4-6, 1999. I was quite desperate.

I now realize that God the Father wanted us to focus, not on the demonic, as Mother Nadine's talks would have done but on the gift of healing. I believe God the Father wants to introduce healing into His church. However, many priests are frightened of this gift of the Holy Spirit.

Many priests have been turned off of a healing ministry because it seems to attract some unstable characters. There have been times that I attended healing services when the preacher would proclaim someone was healed of headaches or backaches, while those in wheel chairs seem to be passed over by God the Father. I have wanted to say to the preacher, "send those people home for an asprin and get down to the really needy."

When we began intercessory prayer three years ago, I realized that our focus had to be on praying for the entire church, Catholic and Protestant alike. Our original prayers were those found on Good Friday in the liturgy of the church. Since then, we have modified the prayers. However, the focus is the same, the need of the church.

Fr. Benson, the associate pastor in 1996 when we began intercessory prayer trained "healing teams." These men and women join the priests in praying over people on Friday nights. Normally, I am involved in praying over people only on the first Friday, in which we have a Mass of inner healing.

The greatest healing I have seen has been in the confessional. Shame is the greatest obstacle for most of us when it comes to healing. It is quite difficult for many of God the Father's children to realize that they are his beloved sons and precious daughters. If we feel loved by the Father, we can endure any cross sent to us.

Some Catholics feel that suffering itself is a mystery beyond comprehension. I have shared with my community many of my own sufferings to make an important point. "We must," as St. Paul tells us, "make up what is lacking in the sufferings of Jesus Christ." Certainly St. Paul didn't mean that Jesus didn't suffer enough. Rather, he meant that our sufferings are joined to the sufferings of Jesus.

I replaced a resurrected Christ behind our main altar with a crucifix. I feel strongly that this makes us all aware that our redemption is due to the sufferings of Jesus on the cross. But it also reminds all of us that we too must be willing to suffer in union with the sufferings of Christ.

Blessed Padre Pio is very special to our Parish. I was fortunate to go to San Giovani Rotundo, the place in Italy where Padre Pio spent most of his life. I carry a relic of Padre Pio with me constantly. He reminds me that the greatest healings in his own life took place in the confessional. He also makes me aware that sufferings are a part of God the Father's plan.

I was moved to tears as I read the story of Jacinta and Francisco, the two visionaries from Fatima who will soon be canonized by the church. After the three children were shown visions of hell and purgatory, they were taught by our Blessed Mother to offer up even the smallest sacrifice for the souls in purgatory. When the children saw a vision of hell, it made them redouble their efforts to learn to pray in order to prevent souls from going to hell. Unfortunately, many Christians today do not believe in hell. Therefore, suffering makes no sense.

Jesus tried to explain suffering to the apostles, "What father will not chastise a son he loves." The message seems to have been missed even by those closest to Jesus. When Christ told the apostles he was going to go to Jerusalem to suffer and die, he had to rebuke Peter who wanted to prevent it. "Get behind me Satan." Jesus told our first pope.

In May 1999 I visited Fatima for the first time. I was privileged to speak to Fr. Valinos, the nephew of Sister Lucia, the remaining visionary from Fatima. When I asked him about the third secret of Fatima, he indicated that it was never publicly revealed, but he believes that it will involve personal harm to the Holy Father and that the Pope will suffer much. The pope could die a martyr.

When I questioned his explanation, Fr. Valinos said that Jacinta had a vision in 1917. She saw the Pope being stoned. "Should I tell the people?" she asked Lucia. Lucia replied, "do not tell them."

I was quite distraught when I learned that mother Nadine could not come to our parish retreat. I called Dr. Mike and Helen Rozeluk on May 23, 1999. I pleaded for him and his wife to come to Slidell for our retreat. I truly believe that God the Father was trying to tell us something important. The healing ministry of the church will be important in the coming times. Helen, his wife, spoke first on Saturday, June 5, 1999. Then Mike shared the story of his healing in Garabandal. Garabandal is not an approved site of apparitions, but many people have been touched there by Our Lady.

Helen Rozeluk

My name is Helen Rozeluk. My husband Michael is a dentist in Toronto, Canada. Because our story is so closely linked to Garabandal, I must first give a short summary of the events of Garabandal.

Garabandal is a tiny village in the Cantabrian Mountains of northern Spain, where the Blessed Mother "allegedly" appeared to four little girls between the years 1961-1965. I say "alleged" only because the Church has still not passed it's final verdict on the authenticity of these apparitions. However, what Michael and I experienced there and since then has really wiped out any doubt in our minds.

Our Lady appeared in Garabandal under the title of Our Lady of Mt. Carmel. Mount Carmel is a mountain near Nazareth. In the early years of Christianity, it was in the caves of this mountain that the first monastic communities began. Today these monks are called the Carmelites. After the destruction of Jerusalem, the monks dispersed throughout the world. In the thirteenth century, their superior general was St. Simon Stock, an Englishman. In the year 1251 Our Lady appeared to him just the way she appeared in Garabandal: she wore a white dress covered with a blue mantle but, in addition to that, she wore a full-length brown apron that hangs off the shoulders. She took this "scapular" off Her shoulders and presented it to St. Simon Stock and said, "This is the clothing of protection for your order. Wear this, My Scapular. Anyone who dies wearing this Mantle will not suffer eternal fire."

Now, if we remember the traditional habits of many monks and nuns, they very often included a long strip of cloth that hung from the shoulders to the ankles, front and back. This is the scapular. However, lay people like you and me can hardly be expected to wear such a thing, so the Church adapted the full-length scapular for ordinary people to be simply two small squares of brown wool joined together with two ribbons or strings. This scapular is worn around one's neck, one woolen square on one's chest and one on the back. When blessed, it also carries with it Our Lady's promise, that whoever dies wearing it shall not suffer eternal fire.

In the Eastern Church, the history of Our Lady's mantle dates back to several hundred years earlier, to the year 921. Our ancestors, Michael's and mine, who lived just north of the Black Sea, used to love to sail down the Dnieper River, across the Black Sea to attack the Greek capital of Constantinople. Our ancestors, the Slavs, were pagans at the time. On one of these occasions in the year 921, when the armies of the Emperor of Constantinople were occupied elsewhere, the Slavs surrounded the city and held it under siege. The inhabitants were very frightened. They were defenseless. The Archbishop of Constantinople gathered everybody in the Cathedral at Blachernae, which housed the robe of Our Blessed Mother, and led the faithful in prayer. In the midst of these prayers, Mary appeared standing on the dome of the church and She spread her mantle over the whole city. This was such a frightening sight to the attackers, that they took off and fled. Since then the Eastern Church celebrates the feast of the Presentation of Our Lady's Mantle on July 2nd.

The significance of this date is the fact that Our Lady's first appearance at Garabandal was **July 2, 1961**.

When Our Lady appeared in Garabandal as Our Lady of Mt. Carmel, it was as though to reinforce the importance to hanging on to Her apron strings. It was also meant to stress that, east or west, Our Blessed Mother is there as our protectress.

The Blessed Virgin appeared to the four little girls daily, many times a day, during those four years in Garabandal: night and day, winter and summer. She led them through the whole village in ecstasy, leading them in the rosary. She especially liked to have them pray before the Blessed Sacrament. She also stressed the importance of praying for priests, going to frequent confession, receiving Holy Communion daily, visiting the Blessed Sacrament often but above all to lead good Christian lives.

The wearing of the brown scapular and daily recitation of the rosary were the constant underlying theme of these visitations. Our Lady taught the youngsters how to pray slowly, concentrating on what they were saying instead of just mouthing the words.

Whenever Our Lady appeared with baby Jesus, the girls played with Him and at one such occasion they tossed little pebbles to Him, hid them in their hair and wanted Jesus to look for them. Our Lady picked up these pebbles and kissed them and gave them back to the girls but said She would rather kiss blessed objects. The people responded by bringing their crucifixes, rosaries, missals, holy pictures, whatever they had and Our Lady kissed them and returned them to their owners. She also promised that, through Her kiss, Her Son would perform miracles and prodigies.

One of these kissed items was a medal, which one of the visionaries, Conchita, subsequently gave to Joey Lomangino, a blind man from New York, who later began a powerful Garabandal apostolate. Wherever he spoke, he would offer for veneration this medal that Our Lady kissed. And Our Lady was true to Her promise: there were many, many miraculous healings through this medal.

What is our connection to Garabandal?

Michael and I both grew up in immigrant Ukrainian families. As a result, our lives were very intimately tied to our Ukrainian community. We both worked in the same Ukrainian youth group, I taught in Ukrainian Saturday schools, sang in the choir, led summer camps. Michael was in the national executive of the youth organization and in 1986 was elected national president for Canada. When our children came, we raised them up in much the same way we were raised. In addition to regular school classes, they went to Ukrainian Saturday classes as well as the usual music and dance lessons and sports activities that most North American children take part in.

Michael's dental practice was very successful. He enjoyed his work. Patients liked him and some would travel quite a distance just to see him. Life was great. Our children, Natalka and Andriy, were doing very well in school. Everyone was healthy. Life couldn't be better.

At that time religion was not a priority in our lives. We were Sunday Catholics. And if something else was taking place on Sunday, then going to church would probably be pushed aside. But God had other plans.

On the evening of February 19, 1986 Michael was returning home from choir practice. He stopped at an intersection, waiting to make a left turn. No other vehicles were going in his direction. Suddenly, a small Volkswagen came careening from around the bend behind him and smashed into him at top speed. The impact was such that our large car was thrown thirty feet forward to the other end of the intersection. The Volkswagen was totalled.

To this day Michael does not remember how he got out of his car. His first recollection is of leaning over the hood of our car and feeling very weak, dizzy and nauseous. When a policeman finally arrived, he charged the other driver with reckless driving. There was also an ambulance station at that corner. The attendants ran out when they heard the crash. But neither they not the policeman thought to take Michael to the hospital. He was left to make his own way home in his own car, which was another half hour along the highway.

The following morning Michael could not lift his head off the pillow. He was one Mass of pain, from his neck to his jaws to his shoulders and down his back. We had to cancel that day's patients and Michael went to see his doctor, who immediately sent him for x-rays. However, if there are no broken bones, and x-ray will show nothing. Michael was simply given pain killers and muscle relaxants and sent home. When things got worse, he was finally sent to a specialist, then another, then another. So began an eight year long procession of visits to specialists, lawyers, physiotherapists, chiropractors, even a psychiatrist. You see, if the doctor cannot find the problem, then it must be all in your head!

Michael could not take any of the prescribed medication. He had bad reactions to all of them. The only thing he could tolerate was Tylenol-3, but it helped very little if at all. He simply ate it like candy. I used to renew his prescription for 100 Tylenol-3 every three weeks, like clockwork.

Eventually, after several years, Michael finally managed to be seen by some top specialists: in Toronto, in Philadelphia, in New York and elsewhere. Finally we were getting somewhere. But the final diagnosis was very discouraging: Michael had damaged ligaments in his jaws and some damaged vertebrae in his neck. He was told to limit his work to one hour a day. His condition was permanent. He could look forward to increasing arthritis in his neck and upper back and could expect to be a total cripple within five years.

Living in constant pain and having no relief whatsoever, one still has to support one's family, pay the bills and put food on the table. This was what kept Michael going, sometimes by sheer willpower. He kept trying to work, but very often someone would have to bring him home in the middle of the day. If he managed to work three days in a row, he would definitely be flat on his back in pain on the fourth day. Sometimes he would faint from the pain. Sometimes it made him vomit. Sometimes it was so intense that he lay flat on his back on the floor for 40 hours, unable to move, unable to eat or talk. He was able to predict weather changes better than the weatherman. That was when it was the worst. Many patients left him. Many understood and stayed but they made a point of calling the office before coming in for their appointments, to make sure he was still there.

For eight years, Michael lost from one half to two and a half days work every week. It doesn't take a mathematician to figure out how that affects one's finances. You still have to pay your staff, your suppliers and your mortgage. There were many times when we didn't know if there would be enough to put food on the table. We lost many of our friends too. When you have to cancel your social occasions time after time, eventually those people stop inviting you or even calling you.

In addition to this, when you're in pain, you still have to put on a good face when you're at work. Then, when you come home, you let it all loose, and for eight years the children and I were like emotional punching bags. I never knew which Michael would be coming through the door that day. His outbursts were unpredictable. Anything could set them off. The children were also affected. But how do you explain to a six-year-old or a ten-year-old that daddy is not angry with them? "Why is Daddy always yelling at me? Why doesn't Daddy want to play with me? Why doesn't he want to pick me up?" How do you explain to a six-year-old or a ten- year-old that daddy is not angry, he is sick. So, for eight years, I was a parent and a half to the children, pretending to be strong.

With nothing but increasing disability to look forward to, Michael also became increasingly despondent. Every week for that eight years, I would hear one of two things from him. One was, "Why don't you take the kids and just leave? You deserve a better husband, the kids deserve a better father, just leave me alone and go." And another one was, "Why don't you go to the garage and get the ax and just give it to me over the head because I can't take it any more!"

To tell the truth, between Michael's outbursts, the desperation, the illness, having to be two people at one time, helping him in the office as well, I was very close to losing it. I could have gone crazy. Either our marriage would have been gone, or I would have been sent to the mental institution. Only one thing kept us from falling to pieces, only one thing, and that was my rosary and Our Blessed Mother. The fact that Michael and I survived this ordeal and that we are here to tell you about it, I credit the rosary and Our Blessed Mother and Her alone. And I thank Her for it every day. Thank you, Mamma.

The rest of this story belongs to Michael. Michael will now share his testimony.

****

Dr. Michael Rozeluk
A Renewed Life

Thank you Fr. Carroll for inviting us to your beautiful parish on the occasion of your Jubilee Parish Retreat and the 40th Anniversary of your ordination.

My story involves the story of Garabandal. So many people hear about Garabandal but they do not hear all of it. They only hear about the Warning and the Miracle. They hear about the strange things that the girls were doing. And people, because they do not understand, are afraid and scared. But Garabandal is a story of love and hope. Yes …love and hope. The love of a mother concerned for Her children and Her appearances where She guides us back to Her Son Jesus. And She gives us the hope, through Her kiss where She said "through My kiss of these objects, My Son Jesus, would perform many prodigies throughout the world." Yes, this is hope. And my life which was so full of despair was renewed in Garabandal. Here is where I found Her love and hope in a most astounding way.

As a result of all this constant pain, I fell into a terrible state of depression with only my family (my wife, Helen, my mother. Irene, and my brother, Jerry) for support. It was total misery, for when I was in absolute agony, nobody could talk to me or help me in any way. I withdrew into myself; life wasn't worth it.

A Changing Attitude

I was not particularly religious at this time, but I found myself changing. This was mainly due to the fantastic support I was receiving from my wife, Helen, and my mother, both religious persons. Suddenly, my mother informed us that she had breast cancer. I talked to her doctor and he said that there was no hope for her as the cancer had spread too far. While I was on the floor in so much pain I started praying. Prayer took on a new form, not just a simple recitation of The Our Father and Hail Mary but it seemed that I started a one-way type of conversation with God. I began to read the Bible and promised God I would read it every night for the rest of my life. I prayed to God and asked that He heal my mother if it was His wish. *If it was His wish!* I made several promises to keep for the rest of my life. There were no conditions! This was something strange for me, because I, like so many other people, want things and we promise things but we set our own conditions. Here there were no conditions. It was up to God. I put my mother, whom I loved very much, and myself into His hands and into His care with complete trust.

It was because of my mother that Helen and I wound up going to Garabandal. She really lived her faith devoting much of her time to the Church and the women's league. But every day while in her pain, she still worried about me and the pain that I was in. And she prayed for me.

After various cancer treatments proved ineffective and the doctors declared that nothing more could be done, my mother was resigned to the fact that she would die. That was in the summer of 1993. Helen and I then decided that perhaps a pilgrimage would be good for her. I knew she would like to go on a religious pilgrimage but that she wouldn't go alone. So I told her that we were planning to go to Garabandal and promised her that we would all go. She was extremely happy but said that she would not be around. In spite of her words I promised that we would go on this pilgrimage.

Throughout September and October of 1993, my mother's condition deteriorated rapidly. It was as if God was testing me to see if I would keep my promises. Now when I prayed, I asked God that if He wished to take her, it was His choice. And take her He did on November 14, 1993. I, of course, was deeply saddened but I missed her. I would have done anything for her just as she would have done for me. I completely forgot about our proposed visit to Garabandal.

The Trip

Shortly after New Year 1994 and our Ukrainian Christmas, I felt something bothering me. I remembered my promise to my mother about going to Garabandal and this thought kept eating away at me. Now I said that the promise was null and void as she was not alive anymore. But "we" also means Helen and myself. I told Helen and we decided to join The Workers of Our Lady of Mount Carmel trip to Garabandal for Holy Week and Easter.

We were to fly from Toronto to New York where we would meet with the rest of the group; but before we left I didn't speak about going to Garabandal...only Spain. Even on the trip to New York I kept saying to Helen that I didn't know why I was going. I wasn't very religious, not the type of person to walk around with a Bible in my hands or to be praying all the time. I mentioned to Helen that we would be the youngest ones there and even brought along a spy mystery novel to read in case I got bored. But boy, was I ever mistaken about the people going to Garabandal! And this trip was the best thing I ever did in my life. It saved my sanity, my family life, my marriage, my career and most important, my soul.

At the airport in New York, Helen and I immediately recognized Joey and Marilynn Lomangino because we had seen countless pictures of them. Rosemarie Melenchuk, the tour guide greeted us but we were too shy to approach Joey. However, we were thrilled that he was on the pilgrimage. I was still uncomfortable with saying the rosary but on the bus through the mountains to Garabandal with the cliffs and sharp turns, I quickly learned to say this most beautiful prayer. It was something to concentrate on.

We arrived safely at the village of San Sebastian de Garabandal and it was just as we had imagined it would be: quiet, serene, picturesque...home. We felt very much at ease there but my pain was with me nevertheless. I had my medication and kept taking the Tylenol-3's like clockwork.

Once in the village, it was announced that we would have a Holy Mass shortly. We went to Mass in the village church and you could feel the holiness of this beautiful little church. Most of our pilgrim group went to receive communion but I could not. I did not feel that I was worthy. I had been to confession some time before but something was wrong and I could not receiver Holy Communion. After Mass I went to confession. This confession was to be a turning point for me because, ever since I had been a little boy, I went to confession in Ukrainian. Here I was forced, because of circumstances, to say my confession in English. It was a confession like no other for me. Now I felt that I could go to communion.

This was an important step for me. Although I was not aware of it at the time, this was exactly what Our Lady stressed so much in Garabandal: to go to confession frequently and receive Holy Communion worthily.

The following day I received Holy Communion. After Mass, Joey gave a talk about his experiences in the village church. Following Joey's talk, Helen and I got in line with everyone else to venerate his medal (kissed by Our Lady at

Garabandal). I was feeling my usual self, pain in my neck, shoulders and jaw. Yes the weather was cold and wet outside. When I kissed Joey's medal - and I cannot explain it to this day - it was as if suddenly all the energy just drained out of my body down through my feet. I can still remember the feeling even today. I was barely able to stand and would have fallen if I had not held onto the pews for support. Helen was kneeling and praying when I got back to our place but I didn't have the strength to kneel so I just sat there. Slowly, my strength returned and then and only then could I think about what happened. The pain was still there. Never before in my life have I experienced a similar feeling. It was not a common fainting feeling. I thought perhaps it was the stale air or that I was overtired. But no...it was none of these things.

Later that day we made our way up to the pines where Our Lady appeared to the girls. On our way back I reached into my pocket for more pain tablets and, so that no one would notice, I swallowed them. Doctors usually tell you to take your medication with food, water or something. But, when in pain, you learn to swallow tablets dry and wherever or whenever you need them.

Bob House, one of our fellow pilgrims, noticed that I took something and approached us. God bless him for this act. We talked and I mentioned my accident and the subsequent chronic pain. Bob suggested I ask Joey to put the medal on my neck but I told him I didn't come to Garabandal for that. I had come for my mother, to fulfill a promise I had made to pray for her. You see, I never thought that anything could happen to me. Why me? There were so many other people here that were much more "religious" than I, and who had more serious problems. Perhaps God would help them but I never considered, even remotely, that anything could happen to me. I came for my mother, to pray for her. I told Bob that if anything were to happen, it would happen anyway but I wasn't going to ask for myself. You see, I still had my "hangups" and perhaps was a little obstinate. My pain continued.

Good Friday was a cold and damp day that intensified my suffering; Holy Saturday was even worse. I was taking my Tylenol-3's every three hours just to be able to move around. In the evening the situation became acute; I didn't sleep all night.

Early Easter morning, April 3, I wasn't able to get out of bed to join the rosary procession through the village streets. The pain was so excruciating I couldn't even raise my head as the villagers, singing the rosary, passed by the house where we were lodged. Now I was taking two tablets every two hours or even less. After two more Tylenol-3's we were somehow later able to attend Mass celebrated by tour spiritual director, Father Thomas Blessin. The day dragged on until finally six o'clock came when I took my last two Tylenol-3's.

The Cure

At eight o'clock, we went to dinner. I didn't feel much like eating but Helen urged me to go. As we entered the inn run by Serafin (the visionary Conchita's oldest brother), Bob House approached me again and asked if Joey had put the medal on my neck. I replied that I hadn't asked him. Bob then grabbed me by the arm and led me to where Joey was standing in the corner of the room and said, "Joey, here's a man with a sore back." Joey, always a gentleman, immediately took out his medal, asked me where it hurt and to guide his hand. I didn't know what he was saying but imagined he was praying. He finished, then said "remember all I can do for you is pray...it is up to God. Thank God." I felt no change at this time and the tremendous pain I was enduring was still there. We all had supper and then left to pack our bags since we were scheduled to depart early the next morning.

Two hours later, after packing, while going to bed, I instinctively reached for my medication. As I reached, I realized there was absolutely no pain in my neck, back or jaw. My neck hadn't felt like this for years. In fact, I couldn't remember the last time I had felt so totally pain free. I said my prayers before going to bed and took no medication, but felt I would have to get up in the middle of the night to take it as the pain would be so severe. At 2:00 a.m., I awoke to go the bathroom and afterwards as I sat on my bed, reached from my medication. But wait, there was no pain. I felt terrific! I was sure the pain would "kill me" in the morning but I didn't need any medication at this time. I took out my rosary and prayed the rosary. I thanked Our Lady and God for these few hours.

I woke up early Monday morning and to my utter amazement, I felt absolutely wonderful. I thanked God and waited for the pain to begin later. My wife, Helen, knew nothing about these wonderful few hours for me. As we got on the bus I waited for the pain, but it didn't come.

Bob House, wonderful caring Bob, came to me as we were getting on the bus and before even knowing what happened to me, gave me his medal which was an exact replica of Joey's and which he got from Joey, and told me to use it daily. He slipped it into my pocket. I have been using it faithfully and have it in my possession constantly.

As the bus made its way to the Santander airport, I realized it would be unfair of me not to tell Joey and the rest of the group about the wonderful few hours I had just experienced. Helen knew nothing of this. Eight hours without pain was just phenomenal for me and I told everyone on the bus about the present state of my health. Helen started to cry.

All the way home I expected the pain to hit me again but it didn't. Our new friends kept coming up to me and asking, "Are you still alright?" "Yes," was my answer.

Helen and I missed our connecting flight to Toronto from New York and had to wait even longer on an already exhausting day. When we arrived home very late, it was cold and raining, the kind of weather that usually kept me in the house. The next day, my office staff members were surprised when I showed up for work. The weather was terrible and they knew that on days like this I would not be able to work. They saw my face, they heard me speak, and they saw my energy and how I walked. They couldn't get over it. Whatever happened to Mike?

A New Lease on Life

Since that time, virtually all of my patients have been amazed at the tremendous change in me. I was like the old Dr. Mike before the accident. I joked. I was happy, I was radiant. Weather has not affected me since then and Helen complains that she has lost her walking barometer. Energy? I have too much for even my staff whom I have managed to exhaust every day since then. I relate the story of Garabandal constantly. Once my assistant said to her mother, "Mike is so happy I can't stand it." You see, she didn't know me before the accident. And I can swing those golf clubs again, cart a heavy wheelbarrow, lift heavy weights and do all those things I could not do for eight years. It's wonderful. It has now been over five wonderful years and I thank God every day.

Since then, Helen and I have given a number of talks about Garabandal and will continue to do so as long as we are able. I thank all those who are happy for me and if it's God's plan that my pain should return even this minute, don't feel sorry for me. I have had one of the greatest gifts anyone could have. I felt very lucky after a few short hours and now, in 1999, after over five years, one can imagine how fortunate I consider myself.

As a result of this unexpected gift, the lives of my family, friends, and patients have all been changed for the better, not to mention the many others who have seen me suffer for years. Helen and I will pray that they, too, will be rewarded and that we'll all be able to witness the great Miracle soon.

To this day I ask, Why did it happen to me? I have no answers. God has graced us to witness so many other miraculous healings (see Internet: www.ourlady.ca) through prayer and the Garabandal medal. Remember that our hearts must open to God completely and we can all do that only by first truly being sorry for all the wrongs we have done to hurt God. Second, we must open the door to the church and come through those doors to His house. And then we must come into the confessional to His chosen one, His representative, His priest and open our hearts with a honest and full confession. He is all loving. Yes, Garabandal is a story of love and hope. Our Mother Mary intercedes for all of us. But you must come with that open heart ...and there is only one way. ...through Her to Her Son. Come as that small child, so full of belief and awe when you go to receive Holy Communion. Think about Whom you are about to receive with all of your heart! He came for you.

Helen and I continue to witness many, many wonderful healings, both spiritual and physical, through the medals kissed by Our Blessed Mother in Garabandal. She has been true to Her promise, that through Her kiss Her Son would perform miracles and prodigies. How long Our Lord will permit this wonderful witnessing to continue, only He alone knows. But I thank Him every day for the tremendous blessing He has bestowed on me.

Dr. Michael Rozeluk

"Let Me Tell You the Rest of the Story…"

With these words, my new friend, Peggy, responded to my hello on the telephone. Peggy had a finally telephoned me after several months had gone by, to tell me something important. You see, Peggy and I had met in Minneapolis, Minnesota in November of 1995, at a dental course. Before that, when I had been suffering in so much pain after my car accident, I was not able to attend any dental courses outside Toronto. Then, after I was healed in Garabandal, Spain in April 1994, I went to Minneapolis for a dental course in Orthodontics.

As I was leaving Toronto, I packed a GARABANDAL Magazine from January 1995 with my story in it. I did not know why I was doing this or why I was taking Garabandal literature with me at all. The purpose of this trip, for me, was not to talk about myself but to listen to others talk about dentistry and braces etc. But when I returned home from the course, I had to tell my wife, Helen, of the strange way I had started to talk to somebody. I told her that this person must have thought I was crazy because the first thing I said to her was totally unlike anything I have ever said to anyone before. It was totally unlike ME! Let me tell you the story as it happened.

Early Saturday morning that November, as I sat in the large lecture room with some 500 other dentists, there were still many empty seats available. There were empty seats all around me and all over the room. Quite unexpectedly, someone came and sat next to me. As she pulled out the chair to sit down, instead of saying the normal customary greeting that one would expect, i.e.: "Good morning….hello…my name is Michael Rozeluk, what is yours? etc., etc., very unexpectedly, out of the blue, what came out of my mouth I believe were the following words: **"DO YOU BELIEVE IN GOD?"** She said "YES" and I continued "because I have to tell you how through the prayers and intercession of Mary, I got well"!

This lady was interested and we began a quiet conversation. I told her quickly about myself and how I was healed in Garabandal. She was genuinely interested in my strange approach and wanted more information. She asked that I send her more material. This I promised to do. She gave me her address and her name. Her name was Peggy McGinty, a dentist from Ponca, Nebraska.

After the two-day course, I left for home wondering why I had approached her in this strange way. Little did I know that God has His ways! But I was still to learn much more and experience His guidance first hand! When I returned to Toronto, I mailed her the requested material on Garabandal.

Months went by and there was no word from Peggy. I thought I would never hear from her again. Just when I had almost forgotten, the telephone rang and the first words were, "My name is Peggy McGinty and we met in Minneapolis at a dental conference. Do you remember?" How could I ever forget? That was the strangest thing I had ever said to anyone! Of course I remembered! I was very happy to hear from her but now she said she was going to tell me **the rest of the story.** Better yet, *Peggy will now tell you her own story and how it fits in here. Peggy, it's all yours.*

Peggy's Story

My connection to the events at Garabandal begins about 3 years ago at a dental convention in Minneapolis, Minnesota where I met Dr. Michael Rozeluk. On that Saturday morning I had arrived late to the meeting because I thought it started the same time as it had on Friday. When I got there, the convention hall was dark because they had already begun the slide presentation so I couldn't see very well. It was a large meeting, over 700 dentists and the room was packed. It took me a couple of minutes, but finally I spotted what I thought was the last seat left towards the back and I carefully made my way through the dark room and sat down.

Besides my seminar supplies, I also had a book with me that I was reading, called "Protestant Fundamentalism and the Born Again Catholic" by Fr. Robert Fox. I put that on the table next to me so I could read it at the break. The reason I was reading the book is because I was considering leaving my Catholic faith because I wasn't convinced it was the Truth. In the several months preceding the convention, I had been praying with a group of Pentecostal friends and they had challenged me about Mary's position in the Church. Even though I didn't have a particular devotion to Our Blessed Mother, I naturally defended Her because I knew that I did not consider Her equal with God or worship Her. Nevertheless, I told (what I thought were) my Pentecostal friends, that if God showed me that Mary wasn't part of the Truth, then I would lay Her down and not ask for Her intercession. So they all gathered around me and laid hands on me and prayed (very fervently I might add) that **"God order my footsteps and put the right people in my path that would lead me to His Truth."** I remember I had tears in my eyes because I truly was seeking the path that led to Christ and if that meant Mary was not on that path, then I sincerely opened my heart to that possibility.

A couple of weeks after the prayer, I attended a Jesus and Mary Seminar in Rapid City, South Dakota and for the first time in my life heard the story of Our Lady of Guadalupe. Now, to give me a little credit, I had heard the title "Our Lady of Guadalupe" before, but I just figured it was some Hispanic thing. Nobody has ever told me about Juan Diego or the Tilma or anything. I was completely amazed. Now, when I look back on that time, I understand that the precious knowledge of the miracle of Guadalupe was held in reserve for me for a time when I would need it in order to stay on the path of Truth and not stray from the protective shelter of the mantle of my sweet and holy Mother.

Within that same time frame, I made the journey to Minneapolis for what I thought was to learn more about orthodontics, **but God had a much higher agenda in mind.** *He had a prayer to answer that would penetrate deep within my heart and soul. God wanted to remove all doubt and to reveal to me that not only is Mary most definitely part of the Truth, but She is the Mother of Truth and there is no creature that can lead us to Christ more swiftly and safely than She.*

Now, back to Dr. Rozeluk (I never can tell a story in a straight line, I think it's and Irish thing). Once I had taken my seat, this man on my right, whom I had never met before, leans over and whispers, "Are you Catholic?" A little surprised by the question, I whispered back, "Yes, but I'm a Catholic on a journey of truth." He replied, "I have something I'd like to share with you at the break." Curious, I said, "Okay." He then proceeded to tell me about the healing of his back injury through the intercession of Mary at Garabandal; how, since then, his faith life has been overflowing with an abundance of grace through the conversions and healings God was manifesting with the medal he had been given that had touched a medal kissed by the immaculate lips of our Heavenly Mother. I was deeply impressed by his sincerity and his humility. We exchanged addresses and phone numbers and I was not to talk to Dr. Rozeluk again for several months.

As I drove the 5 hour long trip back to my home in Nebraska, I had much to ponder and pray about. It really struck me how out of 700 seats in that convention hall I just "happened" to sit next to this dentist who had been healed through the intercession of Mary. Between the Tilma and Dr. Rozeluk's miraculous healing, I now knew that *God had truly "ordered my footsteps"* and I could hardly wait to tell my Pentecostal friends the Truth so they could share in my joy and embrace Mary as their Mother and intercessor.

When I got home, I called one of them on the phone and enthusiastically shared what God had revealed. Imagine my surprise when he said that it was Satan that healed Dr. Rozeluk. I challenged him and said "So, we prayed to God and Satan answered our prayer?" And since he was so into the Bible, I asked him to show me in Holy Scripture where Satan had healed anybody. He couldn't answer me. I then understood that when they laid hands on me and prayed that "God order my footsteps and lead me into the Truth" their hearts were closed to His answer because they had already decided for themselves what was Truth. Well, as you can guess, I stopped praying with them and now pray for them. I'm still a pilgrim on a journey of Truth, *but now I walk with my hand clasped firmly in the Immaculate hand of my Blessed and tender Mother as She leads me in the footsteps of Her Son, my Savior and my God. I have fallen in love with the Catholic Church, the Bride of Christ, and have been given a precious love for the Holy Father, Pope John Paul II.*

Thank you, thank you, my tender Mother for keeping me close to your Immaculate Heart and protecting me from the dangerous path and the snares of the devil. I am forever grateful.

In the Hearts of Jesus and Mary,
Peggy McGinty

Donna Lee...The Rest of The Story:

Some two weeks after Peggy told me this wonderful story, I called my friend, Donna Lee in New York. We talked for a few minutes and then I remembered about Peggy and her beautiful sign. I wanted to share this story with Donna Lee. As I began to talk I said, "Donna, I just had a phone call from a Peggy McGinty"...*Donna Lee will continue from here.*

"What was that name, Mike?" Please say that name again, Mike" "Did you say PEGGY McGINTY?"

"Yes, - Dr. Peggy McGinty," Mike repeated one more time for me.

Mike had no idea how **that name hit me like a bolt of lightning.** How could he know that the mention of a person, thousands of miles away, whom I had never met, would be an arrow of love through my heart. With my whole "being" filled with such joy, I said out loud, *"Thank you, Lord, oh thank you, Lord!"*

I asked Mike to repeat the name, because I wanted to be sure, I needed to confirm once again, what I had already heard. I think I was also buying a little time to catch my breath. Then I began to tell Mike what had just happened.

Many months before I was given a night of intense suffering. As is my practice, I asked, "What would you have me do, Lord?" I was directed to *say a Rosary* for a soul who was being attacked and was in severe danger. I wasn't told the nature of the danger, but it filled me with a sense of urgency and horror. I don't know how many Rosaries I said that night, but the more I prayed, the worse the suffering, This was a VERY serious attack. Sometimes near daybreak, I felt the suffering lessen. Breathing was now easier, peace and a gentle exhaustion made my prayers immediately charge over to ones of thanksgiving. This battle had been won. Before I drifted off to sleep, I asked: "Dear Lord, *if it is Your will* to tell me whom this was for, I would like to know. But even if it is not Your will, I thank you for the gift of this night". Only one thing did I hear... "Peggy McGinty". This was not a common name. Not a name I knew. I fell asleep. Next morning I asked my dear RJ if he had ever heard of this name. He had not.

It never ceases to amaze me how the Lord will not be outdone in generosity. By this I mean:...every prayer is heard...every gift of sacrifice is accepted...every day offered in reparation is received...every offering of our work, play, duties, joy, tears, laughter, communions, weaknesses, are all used in the outgoing work of redemption.

I did not need to have a name...but was given one.

I did not need to know the nature of the battle...but was told.

I did not need a gift of acknowledgement...but it was wrapped in the form of a friend, and the tag said, "I love you my child, and I thank you." The Lord will NOT be outdone in generosity!

And I try one more time to say, "It is I who thank You, Lord."

Donna Lee

The three of us who were involved in this miracle of God's guidance thank Him in a most special way; three people who did not know each other, three people who were almost a continent apart. And yet we are one in Him. We know that He loves us all tremendously. This is His mercy, Hid love, His guidance. He gave Peggy a sign like no other when the first words that I spoke to her were..."DO YOU BELIEVE IN GOD?" And then...how important Mary truly is in our lives! For it was through **Her intercession** that I was healed. **And THAT...IS THE REST OF THE STORY.**

The three of us, Dr. Peggy McGinty, Donna Lee and I, Dr. Rozeluk put our signatures to this document, attesting to its complete truthfulness and accuracy, this 26th day of January, 1999.

Chapter 8
Healing Stories

"The Holy Spirit gives to some a special charism of healing so as to make manifest the power of the grace of the risen Lord. But even the most intense prayers do not always obtain the healing of all illnesses. Thus St. Paul must learn from the Lord that 'my grace is sufficient for you, for my power is made perfect in weakness,' and that the sufferings to be endured can mean that 'in my flesh I complete what is lacking in Christ's afflictions for the sake of his Body, that is, the Church.'" (2 Cor. 12:9, 28,30)[xlvi]
(Catechism of the Catholic Church)

"The church cannot prepare for the new millennium 'in any other way than in the Holy Spirit. What was accomplished by the power of the Holy Spirit "in the fullness of time" can only through the Spirit's power now emerge from the memory of the church.'"[xlvii]
(Pope John Paul, II * Tertio Millennio Adventiente)

Inner Healing
Fr. Richard Carroll

On Friday night at the retreat, June 4,1999, we had a Mass of inner healing. The prayers that we used were given to me by Fr. Al Fredette. A priest involved in Inner Healing for many years. I was fortunate to meet Fr. Fredette at a priests retreat in San Giovanni, the home of the late Padre Pio. When we began intercessory prayer at St. Margaret Mary three years ago, we decided to offer a Mass of Inner Healing every First Friday of the month. The Priests, together with prayer teams trained by Father Joseph Benson, pray over those who desire it after every Friday night Mass. I have included Fr. Fredette name, address and phone number for any priest interested in getting a copy of the prayers used every First Friday at St Margaret Mary, in the Appendix.

In this chapter I will recount our experience in Inner Healing at St Margaret Mary, as well as a physical healing on one of our parishioners who was cured of back problems at a Charismatic Conference in New Orleans. I will also include two of the many marvelous healings that have resulted from the intervention of Our Lady using Mike and Helen Rozeluk.

The greatest healing that takes place for us as Christians is DEATH ITSELF. Although we always rejoice at little signs that God the Father gives us, we never want to lose our focus. As St. Augustine tells us: "O Lord, ... our heart is restless, until it repose in Thee."[xlviii] Heaven is our ultimate goal therefore healing is a temporary remedy. Death is the door through which we pass to go to our Heavenly Father.

Mother Nadine Brown invited me to a conference in Omaha, Nebraska last November. Mother Nadine is the superior of a group of religious women and men called "Intercessors of the Lamb". Mother Nadine gave the conference talks. Each night Mass was celebrated for those attending the conference in a hotel in Omaha.

Inner Healing at Medjugorje in Confessional

I didn't expect to be asked to offer Mass and preach during this week. However on November 15, Mother Nadine requested that I be the celebrant and deliver a homily.

I told the story of Linda Jefferson. I also recounted what happened to me in Medjugorje. In 1989 on one of my three tours to Medjugorje, I was outside church hearing confessions. I sat in the hot sun for more than an hour, yet no one came to me for confession.

Each time I thought about getting up, I recoiled at the prospect of being confronted by Sister Sacristan. "Go back and hear confession," she had told me the night before.

Finally, it was almost Mass time. As I was preparing to leave my post an attractive woman came to the outdoor confessional. When she learned I spoke English, she was thrilled. "I have an eleven-year-old daughter," she began. "She is illegitimate. I was not married when my daughter was born. Every time I look at her I see nothing but my sin," the woman confessed.

I gave her absolution. I then prayed a prayer for inner healing. As I got up to leave, I met her daughter. She was beautiful. "You are lovely" I told her. The child beamed.

The next day the mother sent me a note. "I have been healed... I can love my child for the first time."

Mary Magdalene

I told the stories of Linda Jefferson and the woman in Medjugorje when I spoke in Omaha. A woman came up after Mass, "Father, would you hear my daughter's confession," she pleaded.

I hope the daughter wants to go to confession I thought to myself. The young woman had driven three hours to come to Mass. She was not taking part in the conference. But at her mother's insistence she attended my Mass.

"Father your talk hit home to me" Mary Magdalene said. "Mother thinks I had an abortion, I have actually had 7," Mary Magdalene said. "I tried suicide," as she showed me her wrist.

"Finally after the seventh abortion, I decided I wanted a baby. I had a beautiful little girl. She is now four. But every time I look at my daughter all I see is sin."

After absolving her of her sins, I prayed a prayer of inner healing. I asked Jesus to send any evil spirits that may be affecting her to the foot of the cross, to be bound by Jesus himself. "May Jesus pour over this daughter of mine his blood shed on Calvary," I prayed.

This was an intense moment of Divine Mercy. When I returned to Slidell, I asked her if I could use her story if I wrote another book. I will not use your name" she quickly agreed to let me use her testimony.

I chose the name Mary Magdalene because she certainly knew she was a sinner. But Mary Magdalene experienced Divine Mercy from the hands of Jesus himself. She had an intense love for Christ. When all the apostles ran from the cross, with the exception of St. John, it was Mary Magdalene who stood beneath the cross, supporting our Blessed Mother. What a fitting name I thought for someone who was childlike, and knew she was a sinner....Mary Magdalene. Just as this friend of Our Lady, Mary Magdalene was a perfect example of a sinner being converted and coming home to God the Father. This woman in Omaha had a true "born again" experience. It came to her through the Sacrament of Penance.

Letter to Father Carroll – Free At Last

Dearest Father Carroll,
I have had the strongest urge to write to you since hearing you and speaking with you during my confession at the Intercessors of the Lamb conference in Omaha. I know so many people spoke with you that it would be too much to hope that you would remember this poor soul. But because you showed me God's mercy during my confession of my abortion 25 years ago, and that my son's growth on his brain is not the result of my sin, I feel I must thank you again for bringing me to the Father. How long I

had been lost – how long had I carried the burden of this most horrible sin against the Father.

I did as you said – ask the Blessed Mother to show me my child and to assist me in naming the baby. And dearest Father, she did not fail me. Mary came to me and showed me my daughter –whom she called Clare. At once I was consumed with profound sadness and regret while at the same time I felt great comfort and solace. Mary wrapped me in Her Mother's arms while I wept. I know now that my little Clare is an angel who does indeed watch over me and prays for me. In the silence of my heart I speak with little Clare and have found great peace.

Dear Father Carroll, you were the instrument our Father above chose to help me clean my soul. You're the magnet that brought my heart to His, and the conduit of love which, I know now, will forever bind me to Him. Bless you, dearest monsignor.

I have never had mystical experiences before though I've prayed to the Father and His Son daily for sometime and I do say the Rosary daily, during which time I beg the Blessed Mother to come to me. For years I felt dry. Since my confession and Mary's visit of comfort to me, She has come again. Mary told me that I am to be used as a guide for Her, bringing little children to Her and Her Son. I am to teach them to pray and to love the cross. It is there at the foot of the cross Jesus will enter our hearts, and Mary will stand by us. The miracles from this experience overwhelm me – the coincidences, too. You see, I started teaching first grade catechism this year and had already been blessed with 23 little children in my class. This is no coincidence is it Father? This is part of God's plan for me, isn't it? Mary's words to me were that I had a mother's heart like hers – that because my son suffers, too, as Her's did, I have been shown by Her, the true meaning of a mother's love. She told me to envelope my little one's in my coat of love, hold them tight to my heart and lead them to her. But

Father – how unworthy I am to serve this role! I have the sense in my heart that Mary would like me to begin a prayer group for little ones – and I don't know how to begin. Please guide me Father Carroll – please pray about this so that I do only what Our Mother asks of me, and do it only to honor Her Son. I am just a child myself! How can I possibly lead others, the precious children, to Her?

I pray for you daily dear Monsignor. I thank the Lord for the gifts He has given you, and through you, to me. May God always keep you close by His Heart, and may the Holy Spirit continue to radiate His love for each of us through you.

****

Miracle Stories

Our Lady's Kiss Heals

I was so moved by the many stories Mike Rozeluk told at Garabandal, I asked him to share some of these healings. It is important to realize that these healings in a real sense are kisses of our Lady. We all need encouragement on this journey to the Father. Like St Paul we too "grow weary of doing good." We need to be reminded that there is nothing "magical" about healing. Sometimes the Holy Spirit wants to heal using something as simple as a medal. The Rozeluk's medal contains a small piece of a missal kissed by Our Lady. But I feel that any legitimate healing obtained through the intercession of Mary is a simple sign of a love our mother has for each of us. The first story is that of Angela.

****

Our Lady's Kiss Heals Broken Bones

My story begins on February 20, 1998. I was returning home from the evening shift at work. It was almost midnight. As I was crossing the street to reach my son, who had come to pick me up, a car suddenly hit me.

The ambulance rushed me to Scarborough Grace Hospital in Scarborough (the eastern suburb of Toronto). X-rays revealed that my pelvic bone was broken in three places. My sacral bone (the base of my spine) was also broken but, thank God, no permanent damage was visible. I did not need an operation. However, there was little that doctors could do except give me pain killers and monitor me. You cannot put a cast around the pelvis.

After a week in the hospital, I was sent home with painkillers and a walker. I was not able to place any weight on my pelvic bone or hips. Even sitting caused excruciating pain. Walking was barely possible. I required the help of my family to move about in my house or even to get in and out of bed. I was fortunate that my friend Maria is a registered nurse. She came to my home almost daily to check on my progress and to help me. My recuperation was expected to last several months, since the pelvic bone is the thickest one in the body and has to carry its whole weight.

My friends were shocked at the news of my accident. Soon they contacted Bishop Roman Danylak, who was still in Toronto at the time. The week after I returned home, he was kind enough to visit me and bring me Holy Communion. Then he prayed over me.

One week later, another friend of mine, Johnny, called Dr. Michael and Helen Rozeluk and asked them if they would come to my home to also pray for me with their medals that were touched to Our Blessed Mother's kiss in Garabandal. I had never met Michael or Helen before but I did want to see them after I heard about Dr. Michael's cure and Our Lady's visit to Garabandal. We arranged that Dr. Mike and Helen would come the following evening. That was March 11, 1998.

When they arrived, Maria (my nurse friend) was already there. It took me a long while to make my way to the living room where my son had seated Dr. Michael and Helen. My son's girlfriend was also present. The pain in my body was excruciating. Maria helped me sit down between Dr. Michael and Helen. To relieve the pressure on my hips, she placed a sofa cushion under my feet. We talked for a while. They told me about the Blessed Mother's apparitions in Garabandal, about Her messages, about Dr. Michael's miraculous healing. Then I asked them to pray over me with their most special medals that have Our Lady's kiss on them.

In addition to their medals, Dr. Michael also took out of his pocket a special crucifix that contains a piece of the True Cross. When Maria held it in her hands, she experienced something very special. Because of this, Dr. Michael insisted that we had to call Bishop Danylak immediately after the prayer. During all this, I was half sitting and half lying down and, naturally, in a great deal of pain.

They placed their medals on my hips and pelvic bone. They began to pray. The medals became hot and then the pain was suddenly gone. I cried out that pain was all gone! Helen suddenly asked if I could stand. Without even thinking about it and before anyone could react, I just stood up without any kind of support. My son was still leaning over to get my cane and there I was, standing over him. It is impossible to describe the astonished look on his face.

At this time, Dr. Michael went into the kitchen to telephone Bishop Danylak. While they were talking, I began to walk. I walked into the kitchen all by myself, then into the dining room, into the living room and around again...and again. Everyone was screaming – screams of joy. Of course, Bishop Danylak wanted to know what had happened. When Dr. Michael told him, he asked to speak to me immediately.

I took the phone and repeated to Bishop Danylak what I have just written down. He praised God and gave Him thanks. Then he asked us all to gather around the telephone and we all said a prayer of thanksgiving to God. There were six of us present around the telephone and he, Bishop Danylak, was the seventh. Then he blessed me over the phone and our conversation ended.

As the Rozeluks were getting ready to leave, I felt a sudden urge to walk up the stairs of my house. My son did not want me to try but I knew that I could. There were more screams of joy as I walked up the stairs without even so much as using the handrails of the staircase. I got up to the top, turned around and declared that I have ABSOLUTELY no pain. Then I walked down those stairs again. I cried! We all cried. Dr. Michael and Helen then asked me to have new x-rays taken of my pelvic bone. I agreed.

I went to bed that evening totally pain-free and so very happy. The next morning, when my nurse Maria called to ask how I felt, I had already been up for some time, cooking up a storm in my kitchen after a very restful and wonderfully pain-free night.

One week later, I joined Dr. Michael and Helen at St. Josaphat's Ukrainian Catholic Cathedral for Mass and I walked up the many entrance stairs of the church by myself, with no outside aids. I did have my pelvic bone x-rayed again and my bones have healed normally. I am fine and I thank God continually for my health and that wonderful miracle in my life.

It has now been over one year since this wonderful miracle took place. In obedience to my dear Bishop, I am writing this story and encouraging others to truly believe. Our Lord Jesus does have a most wonderful and merciful heart. His Mother Mary can and does intercede on our behalf many times but we have to live as Our Lady requested and obey God's laws. I thank Jesus every day for

His love and the wonderful gift of Her kiss that His Mother Mary has left on these medals and so many other blessed objects in Garabandal. She promised then, that through Her kiss, Her Son would perform many miracles and prodigies. Indeed, Her words have come true once again.

Amen.

Angela
Scarborough, Ontario

April 20, 1999[xlix]

****

Faith, Trust and Miracles

March 28, 1999

Chances are, I am just like many people you know, a friend, a co-worker or a member of your family. I was born in the Toronto area. I married my high school sweetheart and we were blessed with two beautiful, healthy children: the first born a boy and then soon after, a little sister for Michael which completed our family. In short, I thought we had it all. We are an average family with good times and bad. My husband and I were raised as good Catholics, and we are raising our children in that same manner. I said my prayers before bed and always remembered to thank God for His many wonderful blessings.

In October of 1994, we were shocked when our eight-year-old son Michael was diagnosed with leukemia. Our formerly perfect lives fell apart. We were scared and confused, just hoping it was a bizarre dream from which we would soon awaken. How could this be happening to us? Our son had always been so healthy! As it turned out, it was no dream; it was every parent's nightmare and we were terrified by what lay ahead. We knew instinctively it was to be a true test for our family and for our faith.

At first, it was the unknown that had so frightened us, but as we soon learned, there was very little relief in the details of cancer treatment and, of course, all of our fears were worsened by the reality that it was the life of an eight-year-old boy hanging in the balance. The awful truth was that Michael would need to complete three years of chemotherapy. For the first six months, he was in and out of hospital. He was given chemotherapy daily and three weeks of radiation directly to his head. These six months of intensive chemotherapy were hard on Michael and excruciating to witness as parents. He felt ill most of the time and missing school and friends compounded the problem. All of the upheaval was hard on my husband and me, but we knew it must be unimaginable for our young son. It all seemed so unfair. Michael missed the complete year of grade three. We prayed daily and our strong belief helped us get through the first six terrible months of intensive treatment.

The next phase of the treatment is known as the maintenance phase. This stage was easier on Michael. Chemotherapy was only given to him every two weeks for the next two and a half years. Michael could return to school part time until his strength improved. He was thrilled that he was going to get to see all his school friends again, but a little nervous about their reaction to seeing him minus his hair, since hair loss is a common side effect of chemotherapy. We decided to make his first day back to school "Hat Day". That morning, we arrived at school and when Michael took his first hesitant peek into the classroom, he saw it was "Hat Day" for everyone else, too. He was so thrilled; it was the first time in six months he had actually smiled. Seeing my son's smile after so many months of pain and hardship brought tears of joy to my eyes. I knew then that I would never again take a simple smile for granted!

Throughout this time, we attended church often and prayed the rosary. In my prayers, I asked God for two things: the first - to keep Michael in remission and to never let him relapse; the second was for God to give us all the strength we needed to carry this cross that we were given. It was a hard time for all of us, but through it all, there was my daughter Samantha, our little angel. She was obviously saddened by Michael's illness and she always put him and his needs first. Samantha was only four when he was first diagnosed and, at times, it was difficult to have the time we wanted for both of the children.

On October 14, 1997, Michael completed his last day of chemotherapy. This was a day of mixed emotions because Michael was on his own now. To feel hopeful that the treatments had worked, he would need to stay cancer free for two years without drugs. If he did, he would be considered cured, but if he relapsed he would need more chemotherapy and a bone marrow transplant to survive.

Our nightmare continued, when on January 6, 1998, our Doctors detected that Michael had, in fact, had a relapse, just three months after the first round of treatment had ended. The short amount of time it took for the disease to reappear was not a good sign. My husband and I were devastated, we thought we were going to lose our son. We both started doubting God. Why is He not answering our prayers? After all, we had never wavered in our faith. And hadn't this eleven-year-old boy and our family been through enough?

Immediately, heavy chemotherapy treatments resumed for Michael. He needed to be put back into remission before a bone marrow transplant could be considered. Furthermore, a successful transplant requires a donor with an exact match. Siblings and other family members are tested first, since these are the most likely places to find the high degree of similarity needed for a bone marrow match. Samantha was disappointed that she was not a match for Michael. At this point, a world-wide search began. We were very lost; control of events seemed out of our hands.

Our child's life now depended on the random luck that a total stranger, with the necessary characteristics to match Michael, could be found before it was too late.

I prayed day and night for a miracle. Michael would cry at night, not wanting his body racked with the effects of the radiation treatments. Among the possible effects of prolonged treatment is the inability to reproduce. So, in addition to everything else, we worried that this terrible disease would also rob Michael of the joys of bringing life into the world and, for us, the distant pleasure of being Grandparents to the children of our son. These thoughts upset Michael very much and we continued praying together for a miracle.

With my son's wishes in mind, my husband started searching for alternatives. In doing so, he met Angie. Angie herself had gone though a bone marrow transplant two years before. She began telling us about Dr. Michael and Helen Rozeluk and how they prayed over her with the medal of Our Lady of Garabandal that was touched to Our Lady's kiss. After being prayed over, Angie received such beautiful healing gifts. She suggested that on Wednesday we go to the healing Mass at St. Josaphat's Ukrainian Catholic Cathedral in Toronto.

However, on the day of the next healing Mass, Michael was to be admitted again to hospital for his next chemotherapy treatment. We were disappointed because we were anxious to try this new, faith based alternative to the debilitating cycle of radiation and sickness we had already been through. My husband turned to me and said, "I guess we were not meant to go to the Mass tonight". On being admitted to hospital, a series of blood work was required to tell the doctors if Michael's blood levels were good enough to start chemotherapy. With suitcases in hand, we awaited the results. The nurse came and said, "Great news. There is a room ready for Michael but we still must wait for his test results to admit him". She assured us his results would be fine. An hour later the nurse returned with a strange look on her face, I was quick to ask what was wrong. She proceeded to tell us that Michael's blood levels were too low to start chemotherapy. My husband said, "That is strange. His blood levels should be fine at this time of his treatment." I said, "That's not strange. Someone wants us at that healing Mass tonight!"

We arrived at church at 7:00 p.m. After Mass, Angie introduced us to Helen Rozeluk. When Helen started praying over Michael with her relic medal, I began to cry. After the prayer, she told us to go to confession and then return for Mass on Sunday and have Bishop Danylak also pray over Michael. We did as we were told. We went to confession on Thursday. On Friday, we visited Dr. Michael in his dental office, where he also prayed over our Michael with his medal. Then on Sunday we returned to St. Josaphat's Cathedral for holy Mass. After Mass, Bishop Danylak prayed over Michael as well; it was an overpowering experience. Then the Bishop said, "He will be fine."

I wanted to believe, but I couldn't see any change in Michael, as leukemia is an internal disease. It wasn't as if he were crippled and then could walk. I needed to see for myself some tangible evidence that our long ordeal could be over. So I asked God to let Michael's hair begin to grow back. Well, within days Michael's hair did start growing back in. I was overwhelmed. I called the hospital to see if Michael's hair should be growing. I was told, "Not until six months after chemotherapy".

I knew then that our prayers had been answered. Michael had been cured of leukemia and no longer needed chemo or a bone marrow transplant! We stopped all treatments! Needless to say the doctors thought we were crazy.

It has been over a year now since our last relapse and Michael is still doing great! Our doctor has never seen anyone at Michael's stage of treatment doing so well without chemotherapy. God is a constant part of our daily lives and both our children are healthy. We feel incredibly lucky and know that we have truly been blessed. We know that we need to believe and trust in God's plan for our lives. Miracles DO happen! Michael is proof.

God Bless

N. T.
Ontario, Canada[1]

****

Jerry Dunlap's Testimony

Author's Note: One of our parishioners was cured at a charismatic healing conference. I will let you hear about this healing in his own words.

On January 14, 1982, my whole world changed for the worse. I was working as a machinist in Pennsylvania, when I was involved in an industrial accident. At first, I was misdiagnosed, but after many tests and exhaustive therapy, I was told that I had four ruptured discs. Over the years I had seen approximately thirty doctors and visited several clinics but the consensus was that: 1) surgery was not feasible and 2) my condition would deteriorate with time. The news couldn't have been worse; I was totally and permanently disabled and nothing else could be done. The discs in my lower back were so destroyed that they were literally bone grinding on bone. I had lost most of the range of motion in my neck and legs, and sitting, standing and bending for any length of time caused excruciating pain. Sleeping for the night was impossible. To put it simply, I was in pain all the time and completely miserable.

When my accident occurred I was only twenty-nine years old. It was quite depressing not to be able to do the things that you liked to do. I was very active hunting, fishing, playing golf, and bowling and now none of these activities were possible. At first, I wondered why this injury happened to me. As the years passed and I progressively became more and more debilitated, I prayed for God's grace to help me make one day at a time.

On March, 31, 1995 my world changed again, this time beyond belief. My wife Kathy asked me to attend the Southern Regional Conference of the Catholic Charismatic Renewal in New Orleans. Reluctantly, I said I would go but I really did not know what it was all about. Unknown to me, my wife and her friend Kathy had met the day before. Both felt very strongly that they should go to the chapel at St. Margaret Mary and pray for me to have the strength to go. As they prayed for God to touch me in a powerful way, they asked the Lord for a stranger to meet me and confirm God's love. As the time was getting closer to leave, I wanted to stay home all the more. Actually, along with sitting as one of the many reasons why I should not and could not go, I was giving Kathy a terribly hard time just to get me there. We finally arrived at the conference and as I sat on an end seat, I very matter of factly told me wife that if I didn't like what was going on, or I experienced too much pain, I would go to the car.

The conference began and Father Emiliano Tardiff related his story of being healed of tuberculosis. I listened but kept wondering, "God, why am I here?" As Fr. Tardiff proceeded, he stated that several people were being healed of hearing problems. I watched as the crowd of thousands stirred and several people walked on the stage. Then Fr. Tardiff said six people were being healed of back or spinal problems. At that very instant, I felt a warm burning sensation from my neck down my back all the way to my feet. I knew something had happened, but didn't know exactly what it was. Five people went up to the stage to claim this healing. I stayed in my seat, moving around, testing my back and couldn't believe there was no pain. Fr. Tardiff had another word that people with arthritis in the knees were also being healed. Again, I felt the same warmth rushed through my knees and immediately the pain was gone. My thoughts went from doubt to total happiness. After thirteen years, could I really be healed? As the conference ended for the evening, I arose from my seat and began talking to a friend. Suddenly, a woman of about thirty years of age came up and hugged me. She touched my arm and said, "I know I'm a perfect stranger, but I must confirm for you that you are the sixth person to be healed with spinal problems." It was all I could do to thank her. I turned away from the woman to look toward my wife for just a moment and when I looked back toward the direction of the woman, she was gone. Needless to say this experience was overwhelming and I am so grateful to our Lord. The pain left that night and is still gone. I can move, sleep, and do just about anything I want. But the best thing is to be able to get on my knees to kneel and pray. I hadn't been able to do that for years and years. What a blessing! I was truly humbled.

Just before Easter of 1995, I made an appointment to relay my experience to Fr. Carroll. He was having a sort of down day but said my healing made his Easter and he used my testimony as his Easter homily. One thing Fr. Carroll asked me to do was to go back to my doctor and have him explain why I was healed. I kept putting it off. Well in November of 1996, I had an attack of kidney stones which left me in the emergency room for several hours. After I related my history of back problems to the physician, he ordered several x-rays. Throughout the afternoon, I passed the kidney stone, but the young emergency room doctor still had to speak with me before I was discharged. I brought in my x-rays and slammed them up onto the screen. "I thought you had a serious back injury," he asked, "these x-rays show the back of a young man." He said he didn't understand how a man of forty-two could have the back of an eighteen year old. The discs were perfectly spaced with no sign of injury. Yes, a miracle had indeed occurred and here was the physical proof.

This all has left me profoundly changed. I look at nothing the same as I did before. The physical healing that had taken place was awesome but the inner healing that our Lord has brought since that time leaves me speechless. He is a loving and forgiving God who hears and answers every prayer especially those that are deep within the recesses of our heart and I will be forever grateful for His mercy.

Chapter 9
Mary

"This motherhood of Mary in the order of grace continues uninterruptedly from the consent which she loyally gave at the Annunciation and which she sustained without wavering beneath the cross, until the eternal fulfilment of all the elect. Taken up to heaven she did not lay aside this saving office but by her manifold intercession continues to bring us the gifts of eternal salvation. ... Therefore the Blessed Virgin is invoked in the Church under the titles of Advocate, Helper, Benefactress, and Mediatrix."[li]
(Catechism of the Catholic Church)

"... Mary Most Holy, the highly favored daughter of the Father, will appear before the eyes of believers as the perfect model of love toward both God and neighbor. As she herself says in the canticle of the Magnificat, great things were done for her by the Almighty, whose name is holy (cf. Luke 1:49). ... Her motherhood, which began in Nazareth and was lived most intensely in Jerusalem at the foot of the Cross, will be felt during this year as a loving and urgent invitation addressed to all the children of God, so that THEY WILL RETURN TO THE HOUSE OF THE FATHER WHEN THEY HEAR HER MATERNAL VOICE: 'DO WHATEVER CHRIST TELL YOU' (cf. John 2:5)."[lii]
(Pope John Paul, II * Tertio Millennio Adventiente)

Yesterday afternoon I received a gift of 6 beautiful red roses and I immediately knew what I wanted to do with them. I brought them to the church and put them over by the statue of Our Lady of Medjugorje. I admitted that I have been hopelessly in love with Our Lady since I was 5 years old. I still remember my mother bringing out that old shoebox. Carefully she safeguarded her treasures in it. One was a blue cord. Mom had lost two or three children through miscarriage and finally she had one live birth, my older brother Ralph. He weighed about 3 or 4 pounds and could fit in that shoebox. The doctors gave Mom very little hope that Ralph would live but she took this infant, wrapped the blue sash around him and dedicated him to the Blessed Mother. Somehow I knew that even as a small boy, Mary would always be special in my life because after all she had saved my older brother.

My life changed in Medjugorje on March 25, 1987. Archbishop Hannan had given me a sabbatical for 8 months at the end of 1986. After 17 years as Pastor here, at St. Margaret Mary, I realized that I was not pleasing anyone, not even myself. I felt alone and unloved. I wasn't sure when I left and told the school children goodbye in December if I would ever see them again. I wasn't sure I still wanted to be a priest. I decided I would go to Medjugorje when none of you would be there so I went March 1987. It was the 25th of March when I was standing outside the Room of Apparitions desperately hoping that I would get into that small room in the rectory.

Somehow I was allowed into the room but there was a video camera and newsmen from New Orleans. I didn't want to get caught on tape so I stayed in the back of the room. I knelt down and said the rosary as the two children Marija and Jacov said the rosary. I am not the type that has religious experiences so I didn't expect anything but as they prayed I began to cry like a child. For the first time in many years that night I realized that **Mary loved me.** I realized that despite all of our sins that **she loves all of her priest sons.** It was an extraordinary experience for me. I wanted to repay her in a small way and I borrowed $1,000 and got 1,000 rosaries for the school children. When I got to New York City, they warned us about thieves and before I knew it one of the people in our group had their bags stolen. So, since I was one of the leaders, I turned to two of the people and said "Watch this suitcase. It is filled with 1,000 rosaries." So I went looking for the lost bag. I came back 5 minutes later and said, "Where is my suitcase?" They said "What suitcase?" Someone had walked right up to them and stolen 1,000 rosaries and that case weighed about 75 pounds. I reported it and they said of course there is little chance in New York City that you will ever get it back.

Two months later, while I was still on sabbatical, I received a call from Fr. Gallagher, my Associate Pastor. He said to me that someone had returned the suitcase with all the rosaries. **NOBODY MESSES WITH THAT LADY!**

Our Blessed Mother has appeared to many people in our parish; children, teenagers on retreat in Florida, she has appeared to the young and old. Many are afraid to say it because if you do, they might lock you up but the fact of the matter is there are dozens and dozens of people in this parish who have seen the image of the Blessed Mother as well as the image of angels. It is very dangerous and people who are not childlike really cannot deal too well with that. One of the things that Our Lady has done for me was to allow me to write three books. The advantage is that when you do that, other people have the courage to come forward and tell their stories. I would really encourage Mike and Helen Rozeluk to put their stories into a book form because then people would come out of the woodwork telling them of things that have happened to them.

I had a lady that stopped to see me one day and she said "I have got to tell you my story because I have read your book *The Remnant Church*." And she said "I was raised as a Protestant, my husband was Catholic but I never prayed to Mary and one day the doctor said, 'Your four-month old fetus is dead, it has to be removed surgically. You will have to come have an ultrasound done before we can do the surgery.' During the ultrasound," she said, "I don't know why but for the first time in my life I prayed to Mary. I said, 'Mary save my baby.' All of a sudden," she said, "I was watching the ultrasound and this fetus flipped over completely and started sucking her thumb. Five months later, my healthy baby girl was born. Seven years later, I still wasn't Catholic," she said, "and I went to a Catholic Charismatic Conference in New Orleans and we decided at lunch time to go up to the front of the auditorium. A stranger came up and said, 'tell your husband to go up and pray to with your daughter before the tilma of Our Lady of Guadalupe.' So dutifully my husband got up with our 7-year old daughter. The stranger said to me, 'You asked God the Father for a sign whether you should become a Catholic. He said to tell you this, 'When your baby was dead, you came to Jesus' mother and you asked Mary to save your baby. She went to her son and He saved your child. Your daughter is your sign that you ought to be a Catholic.'" And today that entire family is Catholic.

At the Charismatic Conference whenever Father Kevin Scalan or Sister Briege McKenna come, they always love to tell the story about one of our parishioners. During one of the healing services Fr. Scalan walked around with the Blessed Sacrament and Sister Briege stayed on the stage to pray. As Fr. Scalan passed by, blessing everyone with the Eucharist, a little 9-month old baby girl who was alseep on her mother's shoulder, and had not yet begun to talk yet, raised her head and said "Hi Jesus!" The mother couldn't believe what she heard. She looked at the baby and said, "What did you say?" And she said again, "Hi Jesus!" Nine months old...her first name is Mary. The mother found Fr. Scalan and shared her experience with him and he has shared this story on EWTN and many places where he speaks.

Sometimes there are painful lessons in love that Our Lady teaches us. One of the most exciting things for me happened 10 years ago when Our Blessed Mother cured Kelly. Kelly had taken over exposed herself to carbon monoxide. The doctors said she would be brain-dead when they got her to Jo Ellen Smith Hospital. Finally, on Christmas Day Kelly who was unconscious, heard a voice say, "Kelly, God has much more for you to do." It was her dead brother, Patrick, speaking to her. Kelly came out of the coma unscathed. Tomorrow I will tell you the tragic end of her story. Bad things do happen to good people. There is a lot of mystery in life that defies explanation but I will never doubt the love that Mary has for me and for each one of you.

I would like to share with you just a few thoughts about my trip to Fatima because for many years I never wanted to go to Fatima and after almost 40 years as a priest, I decided I needed to go. I had been angry about Fatima since 1960. In 1960 I was a young priest, just ordained. Every Catholic at that time loved Mary. In 1960 when the third secret of Fatima was supposed to be revealed, the church simply said, "We cannot vouch for the veracity of shepherd children." Historians had said then that devotion to Mary died in the Catholic Church. It died frankly until 1981 when people began to go to Medjugorje. But any way, I decided to go and because of the kindness of a friend, I was welcomed there by a friend of Fr. Valinhos, the nephew of Sister Lucia. Sister Lucia is still alive. She is over 90 years old. She is the only one of the three visionaries that is still alive. I was told that she still sees our Blessed Mother and because of the goodness of the cab driver, who is a friend of the family, we were allowed to see her convent even though it was lunch time. I was invited actually on May 31 by Fr. Valinhos to stay for the Sr. Lucia's 50th Anniversary in Mt. Carmel Convent. She was in another convent for years before this.

Third Secret of Fatima

The most important thing that I learned in Fatima was when I met Fr. Valinhos, I said, "What is the third secret of Fatima?" He said, "There wasn't three secrets. There was only one. The one secret had three parts. The third part has never been publicly revealed." I said that I had read that Cardinal Ratzinger in Germany told the people that the great loss of faith was part of the third secret. He said, "I have no doubt that that is true but there is another part that has never been revealed." I said, "What is that?" He said, "My own personal feeling is that the part that was not revealed is that the present Pope John Paul II will be assassinated. The Pope will die as a martyr." He said Sister Lucia told him that Jacinta, one of the three visionaries who died at a very young age, had a vision of people throwing stones at the Pope. He said this child said to Sister Lucia, "Do I tell everybody?" She said, "No, don't tell them." He said, "I believe with all my heart that the missing secret is that the Pope is going to die as a martyr." Those who have followed the career of our Holy Father know that on a number of occasions, she indicated to Pope John Paul that we are living in times that are not as they perhaps were always before. So the first thing I learned at Fatima was to pray for the Holy Father and to pray for all priests. He is in great physical danger. Also I learned at Fatima that there is a great need to understand the difference between "doom and gloom" and "hope". If you get this clearly in your own mind you will be very much at peace because you have been told by me on dozens of times that the Blessed Mother has wrapped her mantle around this parish. But there are many people who have complained to the Archbishop that all they ever hear from me is "doom and gloom". Unless you listen with your heart, you are going to miss the message of hope which comes out of Garabandal and out of Fatima. Someone gave me a little booklet that says it all, it comes from the World Apostolate of Fatima , it is called the Message of Fatima for Children. It is recommended for grades Kindergarten through Fourth Grade and in this little booklet, it tells you that 20 years after the apparitions of Fatima, Our Lady allowed Lucia, the nun who still is alive, to begin telling people what they needed to hear. Amazingly, one of the most important things she told the children and she showed them, all three of them, was a vision of hell and purgatory. They have seen it, the children of Medjugorje have seen it, the children of Garabandal have seen it, and it scared the living daylights out of them. Was Mary not being a good mother trying to preach "doom and gloom". The way Sister Lucia explained it to the children was simply this, "If God allowed you to see hell you would do every thing in your power not to go to hell and to keep your family and your friends from going to hell." I believe in my heart that the greatest gift that Our Lady has given me is the gift of the heart of a father, but not just any father, the gift of the Heart of God the Father. He tells us very clearly and very plainly in the messages to Sister Faustina, that He does not want to punish but He says punishment is brought on by ourselves. The message of Our Lady to the world is not "doom and gloom", it is "hope".

Sodom & Gomorrah

Do you remember when Sodom and Gomorrah were destroyed, God said if I can find 10 people...first it was 100 people, then 50 people then only 10 people, I will spare destroying that city. He couldn't find 10 and I fear today that Our Lady is trying to say to you and to me "Don't be afraid but do what I tell you to do and the tribulations could be avoided." That is what touched me so much while reading about some of the people involved in Garabandal. When Conchita said to me and to all of us in a book, *The Third Millenium: The Triumph of Our Lady* that the tribulations could be avoided if we do what our Lady asks, that is not "doom and gloom", that is what hope is all about. If you go to 90 percent of the Catholic Churches around the world, and you ask, "Can you tell me about Garabandal, Fatima, Medjugorje?" They will say "I have never heard anything from the pulpit about them." Not one of you here will be able to say, "I wasn't warned."

Many times people get messages and they are afraid to tell them. I received a beautiful letter two weeks ago when I was in the pits after having met with the Archbishop and told that Fr. Joe Benson, my Associate Pastor, would not be replaced. A woman wrote to me and she said in a very beautiful short note, "About three years ago I was told that one Sunday morning one of her friends called her up and said, 'guess what, Fr. Carroll gave one of his doom and gloom sermons today.'" She said, "Oh no, not another one." So this woman said what I did was I just said offhand to God, "Lord what is going on in this parish?" She said "I heard Mary's voice and knew without a doubt it was her. Mary said to me 'He is my Jeremiah, the prophet that tried to warn the people. He is my Jeremiah. What will you do if you are not warned?" It is not about "doom and gloom" it is about a warning. We can prevent the tribulation.

Conclusion

I will close with this, that tomorrow night I am going to talk about the Heart of God the Father because I believe that that is the greatest gift Our Lady has given to me. I wish that she would cure my blindness in my eye, I wish that she would have cured my paralyzed vocal cord, but I knew what I needed and that was the Heart of God the Father, a heart that yearns for his children to return home. If you pray over this picture of Rembrandt's Prodigal Son, you are going to realize something. It is not the ones that are the prodigal children that the Father has to worry about. He can get them home easily. When you are a sinner you know it and it is easy to come home. It is the other one, the tall guy, the older brother, the arrogant good person that goes to church every Sunday. The good person that goes to church every day and is literally tearing the church apart. It is going to be hard for them to change. I just pray that this retreat today that you will recognize now that as we are about to pray our prayer of Divine Mercy. We had to start somewhere and we started with 500 people who were born again Catholic Christians. Everyone of you know now that you are a sinner just as I am, there is not one of you who does not know that Jesus Christ loves you. There is not one of you that does not know that God the Father forgives us that we are saved. Not one of you does not realize the power of the Holy Spirit. You even have something far greater than those Protestants who say, "Are you saved?" You can say "Absolutely, I am a born-again Catholic Christian who has been saved by the suffering cross of Jesus Christ but also I have Jesus in the Eucharist." There is no closer relationship than Christ can be in the Eucharist.

I can tell you just from my own experiences in the community that if you love Mary, the Mother of Jesus, God the Father will look at each one of you as you come to be judged and say, "You are my beloved son, you are my beloved daughter, on you my favor rests." Now please stand and let's pray this prayer together Fr. Stenzel's prayer to be born-again Catholic Christians.(See Appendix.)

Chapter 10
Fr. Richard Carroll
Priesthood

"Hence the priesthood of priests, while presupposing the sacraments of initiation, is nevertheless conferred by its own particular sacrament. Through that sacrament priests by anointing of the Holy Spirit are signed with a special character and so are configured to Christ the priest in such a way that they are able to act in the person of Christ the head"[liii]

(Catechism of the Catholic Church)

"...in virtue of the Sacrament of Holy Orders, after the image of Christ, the supreme and eternal priest, they are consecrated in order to preach the Gospel and shepherd the faithful as well as to celebrate divine worship as true priests of the New Testament."[liv] *(1564)*

(Catechism of the Catholic Church)

"'...and in the sacrifice of the Mass they make present again and apply, until the coming of the Lord, the unique sacrifice of the new testament, that namely of Christ offering himself once for all a spotless victim of the Father.' From this unique sacrifice their whole priestly ministry draws its strength"[lv]

(Catechism of the Catholic Church)

Closing Sermon – Sunday, June 6, 1999

My Dear Children:

Today I am celebrating 40 years as a Priest. It is also a culmination of our Parish Retreat. The purpose of the retreat was to give each of you the opportunity of experiencing the presence of God. For Protestants this is called a "Born Again Experience". In St. John's Gospel, Chapter 3:5, Jesus said, "I solemnly assure you, no one can enter into God's kingdom without being begotten of water and Spirit." For Catholics, the primary meaning of this text is the rebirth we experience in baptism; however, this text certainly does point out to us a need in our lives to experience the presence of God.

For a "Born Again Experience", we must recognize that we are sinners and that it is Jesus who saves us. Our salvation comes through the cross of Jesus Christ. We have seen that salvation is a gift of the Holy Spirit. As Catholics we accept Jesus as Lord of our lives; proclaiming our faith through the Eucharist, and love of our Blessed Mother. It seems to me that there is one additional element to a religious experience – that is a gift of God the Father Himself. Tonight I would like to share with you the lessons God the Father taught me in my journey.

Lessons God the Father Taught Me

Lesson 1 – The Cross of Jesus Christ

It seems to me that I learned very early in life that the priesthood meant sharing in the cross of Jesus Christ. I entered St. Benedict, the minor seminary, in 1946 when I was only 13. I finished St. Benedict in 1952 completing four years of high school and two years of college. I had entered and finished these six years with my brother Ralph, who is now Pastor of St. Clement of Rome in Metairie.

I realize now that God the Father worked very early in my life. I would never have gone to the Seminary alone. I was far too shy. But God saw to it that my brother failed one subject in the third grade. My dad decided that rather than go to the summer school, Ralph would be kept back in the third grade. It was a humiliation to have his younger brother in the same class, but Ralph endured it. As a result of this decision I had my older brother as a protector in the six years at St. Benedict.

I began to have health problems in Notre Dame, the major seminary in New Orleans. Within a few years high blood pressure and eye problems began to plague me. I learned when I was only 22 that I had become blind in my right eye. As I was completing my thesis for my Masters Degree in history, in 1957, I was called into the office of the Rector, Fr. Bolduc. "Archbishop Rummel has reviewed your health records," the Rector said, "and has decided to drop you from the seminary." It was March 1, 1957. I was only a year and a half away from ordination to the priesthood. I made an appointment to see the Archbishop. As this giant of a man entered his office he greeted me warmly, however the conversation was brief. "Son you are not going to live long enough to be a priest. I consulted with the doctor and decided to ask you to leave the seminary."

I will never forget that day. I boarded the St. Charles streetcar and spoke directly to God the Father. "Father I thought I was one of your favorite sons. This is surely a strange way to treat one of your favorites." It was only later that I would understand the scripture Jesus gave us, "For whom the Lord loves, he disciplines; he scourges every son he received."(Hebrews 12:6) It was a rude awakening to know that the priesthood means sharing the same cross His son Jesus carried.

I completed my degree work that spring and got my M. A. in history. I worked for one month at Graham Paper Company then quit. My Pastor offered me a job at St. James Major. With an advanced degree I was sure he would want me to be a substitute teacher, but no, Father Carl Shutten hired me as a janitor for the school and church. From April to August I labored as a common janitor.

Lesson 2 - The Power of Intercessory Prayer

The person I will never forget was Sister Alcanthra O'Carmel.

One day I was coming down the hall with mop in hand. "Richard come into my room please." Another kid must have thrown up, I thought, but I loved Sr. Alcanthra. She had taught me in the 7th grade. As I entered the room, Sister said, "Boys and girls this is the young man we have been praying for. Richard, would you say a few words to these children?" she pleaded.

So with my mop as my crosier, I thanked the children for their prayers. This was the second important lesson God the Father taught me—the importance of intercession of children. By some miracle of grace I was accepted back in the seminary in September of 1957. The prayers of the children were heard. I was ordained after two years on June 6, 1959.

This was an invaluable lesson for me to learn. For seven years now at St. Margaret Mary we have had Intercessory Prayer. Every class has one period a week to say the rosary, sing praise and worship songs and intercede to God the Father for the needs of the church as well as our own personal needs.

In 1995 when I had an acute aortic aneurysm the first thing the children did was intercede for me. Our founding Pastor, Fr. Timothy Pugh had died at age 52 from the same thing. Prior to the surgery the heart doctor explained the prognosis. Half the patients who have this surgery die; significant percentages are partially paralyzed; some never regain the ability to swallow. Yet because of the prayers of these young intercessors at St. Margaret Mary, I recovered almost completely. The only problem I have had is a paralyzed vocal cord.

Lesson 3 - Obedience

On January 17, 1970 I was assigned as Pastor of St. Margaret Mary. I had served as an Associate for five years at St. Francis Assisi in New Orleans 1959-1964. Then Archbishop Cody gave me the job of Building Commission Chairman for the Archdiocese of New Orleans. Later the job of Chairman of the Insurance Commission was added. During these five years I was assigned in residence at St. Rita in New Orleans and Immaculate Conception in Marrero 1964-1969.

Despite the fact that I was a priest for only eleven years, Archbishop Hannan gave me Pastoral responsibility at St. Margaret Mary because of my work in the Archdiocese of New Orleans. **I have been obedient.** After my first five years I was extremely happy at St. Francis. I had raised the money and built the first air-conditioned parochial school in New Orleans. When Archbishop Cody visited this school he asked, "Father how would you like to work in administration?" I wouldn't," I replied. "Good show up Monday morning," he said. I learned the complexity of building and finance. The facilities we enjoy at St. Margaret Mary are due in large measure to the training I received from Archbishop Cody. My obedience was rewarded with this young parish.

My first Sunday in Slidell I celebrated Mass in the cafeteria. I would have Mass in this temporary church for seven years. Meantime I lived in a trailer. I remember saying in my opening remarks; "I am a stranger in paradise." This parish was a gift of God the Father because of my obedience.

Lesson 4 – The importance of Divine Mercy
Mankind's Last Hope

600 adults attended our Parish Mission Friday night and all day Saturday. I had invited Kathleen Keefe to speak on

Sunday, prior to the Mass. Kathleen said, "I don't think it makes any sense to talk about Divine Mercy after everyone has had an opportunity to have a religious experience. They have professed Jesus as Lord of their lives and have been prayed over for the infilling of the Holy Spirit." Why say anything about Divine Mercy after the retreat is already over? "That's because you are now able to be true intercessors." Kathleen couldn't come because of illness. "Tell them Divine Mercy is the world's last hope," Kathleen said. Read paragraph #1588 in Sister Faustina's diary."

> *"#1588 – Today I heard the words: (of Jesus) In the Old Covenant I sent prophets wielding thunderbolts to My people. Today I am sending you with My mercy to the people of the whole world. I do not want to punish mankind, but I desire to heal it, pressing it to My Merciful Heart. I use punishment when they themselves force Me to do so; My hand is reluctant to take hold of the sword of justice. Before the Day of Justice I am sending the Day of Mercy."* Sister Faustina replied, "O my Jesus, speak to souls Yourself, because my words are insignificant."[lvi]

I learned from God the Father that "Divine Mercy is Mankind's Last Hope". The prophetic warnings you have been given are not about **doom and gloom** but hope. Padre Pio put it best, and this is the new vision statement of St. Margaret Mary Parish, when he said "**PRAY, HOPE AND DON'T WORRY**".

Lesson 5 – The Heart of a Father

Nearly thirty years later most of our facilities are built and paid for. We now have classrooms for 750 students, administration, library, cafeteria, band room, church, rectory, gym, evangelization center, and a great amount of paving for parking. Under the direction of Bobby Ohler, our Principal, we will receive the President's Blue Ribbon Award for Excellence in October 1999 in Washington D.C.

We have seen love for Jesus grow by leaps and bounds. Since 1983 we have had Perpetual Adoration of the Blessed Sacrament. For thirteen years we have had Life in the Spirit retreats for our high school students and for the last seven years our eighth grade has experienced the Power of the Holy Spirit. Our love for Jesus has grown as we have come to love Jesus under the title of Divine Mercy. 1800 of our 2400 families have had their homes consecrated to Jesus under the title of Divine Mercy.

For fifteen years I have enjoyed sharing our faith with adult converts. We have averaged between 20 and 25 adult converts a years. Recently a couple came to visit from Ohio. Tom and Glenda House told how their fifteen-year-old daughter who was with them in my first RCIA remembers me. "She was only 15 and giving us some problems when you took her to lunch," Tom said. "You let her drive your red Camaro. She said to tell you she loves you and that was the highlight of her life," her dad said. Now she is married and has three children.

In many respects the best gift I have received as a Priest is the heart of a father. But not just any father, God the Father has given me his own heart.

Kelly's Funeral

Wednesday, May 26, 1999 was perhaps the most difficult day of my life. I had the difficult task of burying a young woman, Kelly, who committed suicide at the age of 29. Kelly was beautiful, intelligent and had a wonderful job at Tulane University. Since she was 7 years old Kelly was the light of my life. Kelly suffered from a mental disorder, manic depression. Over the years I have seen other fathers burdened by the suicide of a child. I never knew a human heart could hurt as much as mine did as I saw her coffin go into the ground. I felt like Abraham when he was asked to sacrifice his only son Isaac, but I believe I was given the gift I prayed for at Fatima, the Heart of God the Father.

On May 13, 1999, I was in Fatima, Portugal. It was here that our Blessed Mother had appeared to three children in 1917. Our Lady woke me up at 4:00 am. In addition to praying for each of you my children, I had asked God the Father for three things, the cure of my eyes (I am blind in one eye and have cataracts on both eyes), the cure of my voice and the heart of God the Father. Our Lady spoke to my heart, "I can get you only one of these three, which do you wish?" I asked for the heart of God the Father. Mary seemed pleased.

When I visited the church where the three visionaries, Jacinta, Francisco and Lucia were baptized in Fatima, Portugal, I was told of a 15th century statue in the rear of the church. When I went to the back, I found to my amazement, a copy of the painting of Rembrandt's Prodigal Son. This is the same picture over our Altar of Intercession on my right. I knew immediately that having the Heart of God the Father would be the key to my understanding of Fatima and the times in which we live. God the Father has such an intense love for His children that He will do whatever is necessary to bring them home to Him.

At Kelly's funeral I spoke about Rembrandt's painting. Prior to leaving for Fatima, someone gave me an incredible book by Father Henry Nouwen, entitled "The Return of the Prodigal Son". This book opened my eyes to understand how God the Father feels about his children. I would like to share a few words of my homily about my precious daughter, Kelly.

Sharing at Kelly's Funeral

God the Father is seen as a half-blind old man. I can now see Father, your infinite compassion, unconditional love and everlasting forgiveness. In the painting, the old blind father reaches out to all humanity. The old man seems to have cried an ocean of tears as he got caught up in our anguish and agony. I know the Heart of that Father burns with an immense desire to bring his children home. Father, I beg you today, welcome Kelly home.

I know Father, it is not your desire to punish your children. They have punished themselves by their own inner and outward struggle. Father it is your desire to let your children know that the love they searched for in such distorted ways has been, is and always will be there for them. It is only in you Father, that we can find **UNCONDITIONAL LOVE**. Give that love to Kelly.

So often Father, we have asked ourselves how am I to find God? The question would better be put, "How am I to let myself be loved by God the Father? Father Nouwen points out that it is we who are doing the hiding. Kelly's search is over, Father, you have found her.

Father Nouwen explains it this way; "Here lies the core of my spiritual struggle." The priest said, "the struggle against self rejection, self contempt and self loathing is a very fierce battle because the world and its demons conspire to make me think about myself as worthless, useless and negligible. The real sin," Father Nouwen concludes, "is to deny God's first love for me, to ignore my original goodness. The parable of the prodigal son is a story that speaks about a love that has existed before any rejection was possible and that will still be there after all rejection has taken place."

Heavenly Father, you alone know the intense struggle for self worth that Kelly experienced. No matter how many of us told her how beautiful she was, how intelligent, how much we loved her, Kelly could never accept it. Father you alone can give us unconditional love.

I share the pain of a father whose heart is deeply wounded by the suicide of his precious daughter in order to make an important point. **No matter what happens to you in life, always remember that only God the Father can give you unconditional love.** If you open your ears and your hearts, you will hear Him say, "You are my beloved son...you are my precious adorable daughter...on you my favor rests."

Conclusion

God the Father has taught me four painful lessons:
1) The need to carry our cross.
2) The importance of Intercessory Prayer.
3) The importance of Obedience.
4) The Gift of having the Heart of God the Father.

In many respects the best gift I have received in my 40 years of priesthood is the heart of a father, but not just any father, God the Father has given me his own heart. As a consequence, I have a great love for Jesus, His Son. The beauty and love of Mary, the Mother of Jesus, mesmerize me. Through my worst trials, I have heard the voice of Mary reassuring me, "As long as I am near you what do you have to fear?"

The great sacrifice of the priesthood was not pleasure or companionship, it was that I always wanted children. God the Father has given me thousands of children that I hold close to my heart. Each of you, regardless of your age or your accomplishment, have your father's eyes...you have my eyes. The love of you, my children, have sustained me in my sufferings as well as in my triumphs.

When Archbishop Hannan appointed me a Monsignor, I was grateful for that honor to our community, but I told you my children, I have worked too hard being a father to give up that precious title. I will not tolerate being called Monsignor, simply call me Father.

In conclusion, St. Paul put it best when he wrote that "You may have ten thousand tutors; but you have only one father in Jesus Christ. It is I who begot you."

On my 40th Anniversary, one of my precious daughters, Christine Kelly, will sing a song entitled "My Father's Eyes" by Amy Grant. I want every one of my children to know that you have my eyes; but I want you also to know that you have the eyes of their heavenly Father. Listen to the words of that song:

I may not be every mother's dream for her
little girl,
And my face may not grace the mind of every one in the
world.
That's all right as long as I can have one wish I pray
When people look inside my life,
I want to hear them say...
She's got her father's eyes, he father's eyes.
Eyes that find the good in things when good is not around,
Eyes that find the source of help when help just can't be
found.
Eyes full of compassion, seeing every pain.
Knowing what you're going through and feeling it the
same,
Just like my father's eyes, my father's eyes, my father's
eyes
Just like my father's eyes, my father's eyes, just like my
father's eyes.

End of Retreat

Our parish retreat ended on a high note. Following the 7:00 pm Mass on Sunday, June 6, 1999 I greeting everyone at the altar. I received more hugs that night than I ever can recall. It was a fitting climax to 40 years of the priesthood.

In putting together this short parish retreat book. I realized that I am deeply in debt, in my journey to the Father, to Fr. Nouwen, for his book *The Return of the Prodigal Son,* and to Fr. Joseph Breault for his work *Seeking Purity of Heart.* I would not have had the courage to try to find God the Father without these guides. I discovered that God the Father found me.

There are three remaining chapters to this book. In Chapter 11: Seeking Purity of Heart, we learn to importance of total surrender to the Father. Jesus himself summarized this for us, "thy will be done." You discover when you have absolutely nothing left to lose, God the Father will find you. Purity of heart is a road marker on the journey to the Father.

In Chapter 12: A Journey to the Heart of the Father, we explore another sign to look for. The Father loves to play hide and seek with his children. The Father often hides from us in the most unlikely places, his retarded children. I will share the story of Martin, a retarded man.

Many of the parishioners of St. Margaret Mary Church have come to love this retarded man, particularly the children. He sings in two or three choirs on Sunday, yet he cannot speak.

"Father, show yourself I beg." But Jesus is trying to teach us to love those who seem to be totally unlovable. The last time Jesus came into the world as a baby; you don't think the Father would send his son to us disguised as a retarded person do you? St. Paul said, "God chooses the weak to confound the wise."

Chapter 13, the final chapter, is about the Triumph of the Immaculate Heart of Mary and the Return of God the

Father. The triumph of Mary will be accomplished through intercession. For three years our parish has engaged in Intercessory Prayer, joining our prayers with that of Our Lady for the world. The side altar is designated as an altar of intercession where we have placed pictures of our parishioners, the Holy Father and the Bishops and Priests in this Archdiocese.

What is Mary asking of God the Father? What is her intercession all about? Our Lady wants to present to God the Father all of his children. Mary wants the prodigal children to return to the Father. Mary also wants the older brothers and sisters to fall in love with God the Father.

The greatest joy of Our Lady will be more than the defeat of Satan. Her deepest desire is to introduce you and me to God the Father. Her triumph is one of **intercession**. Mary wants to hear God the Father say to each of her prodigal children that return home: "You are my Beloved Son, You are my Precious daughter, on you my favor rests."

The journey to the Father is more than a born again experience. It is a moment when we experience total, unconditional love that can only come from God the Father. The old Baltimore catechism put it this way:" your purpose in Life, is to Know God, to Love God and to serve God and to be Happy with Him in Heaven."

Chapter 11
Seeking Purity of Heart

We have shared with you many of the components of our journey to God the Father. In order to be open to this gift of the Father, we must have the proper disposition of soul. Purity of heart is essential to our openness to a religious experience.

The journey to God the Father is a desert experience. Like Moses we are called to strip ourselves of everything before approaching the Father. Moses heard God tell him to take off his shoes, when he obeyed, God revealed himself in a burning bush.

The first step is this journey is a call to conversion. This means a complete turning back to God. If you recall the sharing of Linda Jefferson, that was her experience of returning to the heart of the Father. Jesus himself promised his disciples this gift, "Blest are the single-hearted for they shall see God."(Matthew 5:8)

Purity of heart is what happens to us when God's love purifies us. We become a new creation. St. Paul speaks of this new creation. He says, "... if anyone is in Christ, he is a new Creation. The old order has passed away; now all is new!"(2 Corinthians 5:17) Purity of heart is the fulfillment of the plan of Christ to give our heart to God the Father. "Thy will be done!" This is Jesus' plan for us to reach the Father.

In 1994 I was given a wonderful book entitled *Seeking Purity of Heart* by Fr. Joseph Breault. The subtitle says it all, *The Gift of Ourselves to God.* As a result of reading this book, my own desert experience began. It resulted on March 14, 1994 with 1200 adults coming for confession. The most remarkable experience for me was the gift from the Father of seeing myself as he sees me.

Our Blessed Mother was the instrument used by God the Father. This gift is called "the illumination," or seeing yourself as God sees you. Mary spoke to my heart the way a mother would converse with a child. "Your greatest sin," Our Lady said, "is that you are ashamed of being a priest. When you are ashamed of your priesthood, you are ashamed of my son Jesus." Then she said something that was like an arrow that wounded my heart. "When you are ashamed of my son, you are ashamed of me, your mother." I wept like a baby.

This journey to the father is always through Jesus, who said, "I am the way, the truth and the life;..."(John 14:6) We follow Jesus, the way, as our guide. We seek Jesus, the truth, in the midst of our anxiety. We fall in love with Jesus, the life, even as we wade through our sinfulness.

Mary is our guide. She gave us the example. When told by the angel Gabriel that she was going to be the mother of the messiah, she said, "I am the servant of the Lord. Let it be done to me as you say." (Luke 1:38)

Fr. Breault gives us a powerful tool for giving our hearts to God the Father. In his book *Seeking Purity of Heart* Breault tells us that St. Bernard, the great 13 century mystic wrote of the progressive giving of our hearts to God the Father:
   A. Growing in self knowledge
   B. Growing in compassion for our sisters and brothers
   C. Purity of heart in knowing God
   D. And giving ourselves to him[lvii]

Growing in Self Knowledge

Breault writes, "... No one is able to make the journey by the power of the Holy Spirit alone. ... The first provision for the journey, then, is to be a committed member of a Christian community in an active way." "It means breaking down that interior resistance and hardness of heart which is called "self-will,' ... This self-will, a deep impurity of heart, is inseparable from fear, anxiety and spiritual slavery."[lviii]

As Fr. Breault says, "A radical commitment of our hearts is necessary to follow Christ and live in His body. Jesus said: 'if any man comes to me, without hating his father, mother, wife, children, brothers, sisters, yes and his own life too, he cannot be my disciple.' (Luke 14:16)." As Breault explains "Jesus is not asking for 'hate,' but for total detachment, renouncing all that we hold dear so that we can cling fully to him."[lix]

You recall in the testimony of Toni Hernandez, she shared of her willingness to give up Katie, the child she loved so much, in order to do the will of the Heavenly Father. My own experience of having to give up an attachment to Kelly, who committed suicide, brought the lesson painfully close to my heart. Its only when we have nothing that we can have everything. Toda...nada! The journey to the father involves **total detachment**.

"Real freedom" the author writes "means letting ourselves be deeply touched by God himself."[lx] A "born again" experience does just that.

Often the greatest obstacle to self-knowledge or humility is low self-esteem. In many of the cases of suicide that I have been involved in, the person simply could not accept the fact that they were loved by God the Father. Having a good self-image is a gift from God the Father himself. If you imagine yourself as a little child sitting on the father's lap, let him tell you how much he loves you. If you listen to the heart of the Father, he will say to you...you are my beloved son...you are my beloved daughter. Many people need to repent of their self-hatred. When you do that you will fall in love with God the Father.

Knowing Others - Personal Relationships

The "... second step is knowing others, which is done in compassion. ... When we first know ourselves and then know others, we are led to mercy. Knowing ourselves helps us to grow in sensitivity and compassion ..."[lxi] The story of the woman who had seven abortions was meaningful to me because I too see myself as the prodigal son, just as she did. As a priest I can minister Divine Mercy in the confessional, because I know that I am a sinner.

I am filled with the joy of the Lord when someone is able to unburden their hearts after a long struggle. If I did not see myself as a sinner, I would be like the older brother in Rembrandts' painting; the self-righteous priest would say to himself, "how in the world could someone do something so sinful as to have 7 abortions?" Because I know myself, I can be a compassionate confessors. Confession is a way of my being used by the Father to welcome home his little girl that he finds so adorable. Incidentally Sister Faustina in her diary on Divine mercy tells us that those priest involved in divine mercy will be given the gift of touching hardened hearts.

Purity of Heart in Knowing God

The third step to intimacy with the Father is – knowing God through prayer. "We need to seek his will with all our hearts, not asking him to 'rubber stamp; our plans. ... Instead, he calls us to abandon ourselves to him." Fr. Breault says: "Abandonment is asking God before we have decided: 'Lord, what is it you would have of me?"[lxii]

"Being in love with God is what our life with him is all about."[lxiii] Here is a key point that the author makes, "Falling in love with God is his gift to us that makes us desire to be empty so he can fill us."[lxiv] St. James say "... the spirit which he sent to live in us wants us for himself alone."(James 4:5)

Fr. Breault concludes by saying: "He (the father) desires to give us the gift of purity of heart daily as we enter into his presence, so that we might be in his presence with our whole heart, and allow him to reclaim us, and to deepen and purify our love for him. As we confess our helplessness to God, having only him as the foundation of our lives, we rest and are comforted in him alone."[lxv]

Now you can understand a little better the importance of Perpetual Adoration of the Blessed Sacrament. Prayer is a necessary component for an ongoing conversion experience. The danger with the born again experience is that once a conversion experience is given, it has to be nourished by constant prayer. As Fr. Breault says: "Jesus wants to draw us into the love of his Father by having us drink of the Spirit. He gives us his own Spirit to eat and drink in his Body and Blood."[lxvi]

Catholics are so fortunate. We have all the necessary components to make Jesus the Lord of our lives. The sacraments allow us to deepen our personal relationship with Jesus Christ. Our Blessed Mother is our guide. Once we have experienced the presence of the Father, we have to nourish that gift by intimacy which comes only through prayer. It is all a gift of the Holy Spirit.

Giving Ourselves to the Father

The fourth step in this journey is giving ourselves to the father completely. "The test of our commitment" according to Breault, "is in saying, 'Come, Lord Jesus, come and rule in my heart,' in wanting the fire of Pentecost to be cast on the earth, in wanting fire and the Spirit to be cast into our hearts. We know that to be purified will hurt."[lxvii]

This final stage of intimacy will bring us to the Father. It involves emptying ourselves of the love we have for the cross . We can boast only of Jesus and him crucified. The prayer of Fr. Breault summarizes this gift we seek of intimacy with the Father. "Come Holy Spirit, come and purify our hearts. We desire to be purified. We want to die so we can live in you and you can live in us. We want to be faithful, to return to covenant faithfulness, for in faithfulness we will know you."[lxviii]

As you heard the testimony of our speakers, you realize how integral the cross is to our journey to the Father. Jesus gave us the example of emptying himself of his divinity, in order to save us. In our journey to the Father this is the most difficult part of the trip. Imagine yourself standing under the cross of Calvary next to Our Blessed Mother. Ask her for the grace never to run from the Cross. In 1994 as I was going through this purification process, my prayer to Jesus was for the grace never to run away again. Every prodigal child runs from the cross. "if there is no one left to stand next to Mary under the cross," I prayed, "let it be me!"

Conclusion

Fr. Nouwen's book, *The Return of the Prodigal Son*, and Fr. Breault's book, *Seeking Purity of Heart* were invaluable tools. They have opened up my heart to understand a little better this journey to the Father. I would highly recommend both works.

I could relate to this priest when he said that many of us are shocked to learn that we are sinners. I still remember telling my spiritual director in the major seminary that: "its easy to be a saint, you make up your mind and you do it." God the Father really had a big laugh over that one. It is the broken spirit that allows the Holy Spirit to purify our hearts and draw us into his love. I speak as a wounded healer, who has known and experienced my own sinfulness.

There is no doubt in my mind that I cannot earn my own salvation. It's a free gift of God the Father.

Breault is correct when he says that, "the freedom of the Spirit is released as we rely on God's power in our weakness instead of our strengths."[lxix] I lived through an era that priests were judged as being spirit filled or not. I often wondered what litmus test they used; but I always came up empty.

The Importance of Purity of Heart

Fr. Breault summarizes the importance of purity of heart: "God's solution to our impurity of heart is the purifying force of the Holy Spirit working both in prayer and in daily community life. It is the sacrament of the cross."[lxx]

Fr. Breault puts it this way, "Purity of heart is the beginning of integration within ourselves. Being freed from the necessity to serve our own unyielding will, ... we begin to know the freedom and love of God's will."[lxxi]

Our journey to God the Father is an exciting trip. We pray in a special way for each of you readers, that the Father will give you the gift of purity of heart. May our Blessed Mother be your guide in this journey to the heart of the Father. May the Holy Spirit fill you with joy. May Jesus be your way, your truth, and your life. One day we will be together in heaven where the Father's will is always done! It is there that you will finally realize that **only God the Father can give you the unconditional love you crave.** You will then know for certain that you truly are his beloved sons and his precious daughters. On you his favor rests.

Chapter 12
A Journey to the Heart of the Father

"In the Lord's Prayer, 'thy kingdom come' refers primarily to the final coming of the reign of God through Christ's return. But, far from distracting the Church from her mission in this present world, this desire commits her to it all the more strongly. Since Pentecost, the coming of that Reign is the work of the Spirit of the Lord who 'complete[s] his work on earth and brings us to the fullness of grace.'"[lxxii]

(Catechism of the Catholic Church)

"In the revealed text it is the Heavenly Father himself who comes to us in love and who dwells with us, disclosing to us the nature of his only-begotten Son and his plan of salvation for humanity"[lxxiii]

(Pope John Paul, II * Tertio Millennio Adveniente)

He is retarded; his name is Martin. He cannot speak clearly. He can spell his name M-a-r-t-i-n. For over a year now he comes to Mass at least twice on Sunday; frequently he comes during the week. Martin has learned to come forward at communion time, bow his head and receive a blessing.

Its not that he doesn't try to speak. He learned that the choir would speak over the microphone and say "mic check". He would then repeat these words but they were always garbled.

Finally, God the Father decided to reveal a little of himself to me. I learned that Martin was baptized a Catholic, but he never received Holy Communion. Martin would regularly come into the confessional, he would get a blessing and leave content. However, God the Father wanted more for him.

I asked one of the regular women around St. Margaret Mary Church if she would show Martin the movie that we show to seven-year olds. I told this beautiful lady that as long as he knows communion is Jesus that is sufficient for him to make his first communion.

Martin Received First Communion

On Saturday, June 26, 1999, there was Martin at the early Mass sitting proudly next to this beautiful lady. Heavenly Father, I will give Martin communion, but I need a sign...something in scripture today.

The first reading was the story of Abraham and Sarah. The Father sent an angel who promised this elderly couple a son. However Abraham and Sarah were both 90 years old. But the Father made a promise to the couple through the angel, "... your wife Sarah is to bear you a son,..."(Genesis 17:19) The old woman laughed.

Why did she laugh? The angel asked: "Is anything too marvelous for the Father to do?"

Well I thought to myself, if God the Father can give a son to a ninety-year old couple he can certainly let Martin understand the meaning of communion.

The responsorial song was a little clearer. "The lord has remembered his mercy. His mercy is from age to age on those who fear him."(Luke 1:50) Fear and mercy seem to be little like water and oil. "Do they really mix father" I asked?

It was Matthew's gospel that I received the sign I was looking for. A centurian had sought Jesus out and begged him to cure his son. "I will come and cure him" Jesus answered. "Sir, I am not worthy to have you under my roof. Just give an order and my boy will get better." Jesus was amazed at his faith. "Go home. It shall be done because you trusted." The boy got better at that moment. (Luke 8:5-13) These are the same words that the priest says at Mass before distributing holy communion:" Lord I am not worthy"

That morning a retarded man received Jesus for the first time. "Put your tongue out," I told Martin and when I say "the body of Christ," say amen. The balding old retarded man put his tongue out, and maybe it was my imagination but I thought I heard his angel answer clearly "amen"!

God the Father Hides From His Children

Martin and the beautiful lady who helped him came in to see me after Mass to thank me. Someone had given me a beautiful framed picture of our Blessed Mother. There was still a bow on the picture. When I gave him the picture Martin said. "Mother ...dead." "Now you have another mother Martin," I said. "This is Mary the Mother of Jesus. She is your mother now." "Mother ...dead," Martin repeated. The words were very clear. "This is the mother of Jesus, Mary," the beautiful lady said. I just wanted to say to God the Father, "Father please stop hiding and let Martin speak plainly."

Earlier during Mass, I had explained how many women had been praying for Martin to receive Holy Communion. I asked God the Father to let Martin speak plainly as a gift to us.

A Hospital in 1994

I remembered an encounter I had with God the Father in 1994. I was in the hospital praying. "Heavenly Father," I said, "I feel I know Jesus, the Son of God and my Lord. I also know the Holy Spirit. I have encountered his presence. But I just want to know you, Father. Show me the Father," I pleaded.

Then I remembered the scripture: Philip said to Jesus, "Lord show us the Father and that will be enough for us." "Philip, after I have been with you all this time, you still do not know me? Jesus replied. "The father and I are one."(John 14:8-9) Then I remembered the words of Christ in another place, "I assure you, as often as you did it for one of my least brothers, you did it for me."(Matthew 25:40)

I began to understand. God the Father hides behind the least of his children. "If we saw the Father we would be overcome with ecstasy," I thought. At that moment an orderly came in to pick up the bedpan. This humble black woman was filled with joy. What a terrible job. The words of Jesus rang in my ears, "I assure you, as often as you did it for one of my least brothers, you did it for me."(Matthew 25:40) I thought, "Father are you still hiding?" I wanted to ask the woman if she had seen the Father lately.

Experiencing His Presence

Perhaps Fr. Nouwen, by working with the retarded, had made the connection. God the Father is hiding behind these retarded that he works with in Canada. "Show yourself Father," I pleaded, "show me the heart of the Father and it will be enough."

Our parish retreat was the beginning of understanding God the Father. If we want to find the heart of the Father it involves certain key elements.

We have to learn to be like Alan Fries...like little children. This journey to the heart involves suffering. Linda Jefferson illustrates this point.

The journey to the heart of the Father involves seeing ourselves as Rembrandt did in his picture *A Sinner*. It means seeing ourselves as a sinner even if we seemed on the surface never to have left the Fathers house. Perhaps we are like the older brother. We have secretly envied the prodigal and his sins. When we worked the fields were we filled with resentment? When the father summons us will we join the celebration or like the older brother stay outside?

Seeing ourselves as sinners makes it easy to accept Jesus as our Lord. However, there is more. Are we willing to take up our cross daily and follow Jesus all the way to the cross? Ted Besh and Toni Hernandez showed in their testimony that the cross comes in different sizes. Both of these testimonies show us the need for **total abandonment**.

Our Blessed Mother is a shortcut to the heart of God the Father. If you truly love Mary, she will be the one to introduce you to the Father. God the Father has an incredible love for this woman. He is going to allow her "to crush the head of the serpent".

We learned from Fr. Gallagher and Bernie McClelland the importance of Perpetual Adoration. Sometimes the Father hides behind his son Jesus. If you want to reach the heart of the Father, spend time in adoration of the Blessed Sacrament.

Healing - The Hidden Presence of the Father

I didn't understand at first what healing had to do with a religious experience. Why didn't the Father allow Mother Nadine to come and help us put on the armor of Jesus Christ as we fight the demonic?

I learned from Dr. Mike and Helen Rozeluk openness to the will of the Father. Mike and Helen carried a heavy cross for 8 years when he was injured in a car accident. But once Mike was healed, they didn't sit on the sidelines of life and say to the Father, "life is good, just let us enjoy it."

This young couple has gone out to share their story of healing. To touch others with a medal that contains the kiss of Our Lady on a piece of paper. They don't pretend to be healers. They just want to do the Father's will. They share their story and healings happen.

Perhaps there has never been a time in which we need the healing touch of the Father as much as today. Faith is at an all time low. Will St. Margaret Mary Church be used as a remnant church? I surprised some by saying I don't know.

I realized the hardness of my own heart to the will of the Father when I had to bury my precious daughter, Kelly who committed suicide. "Father, how could you take the last piece of my heart and tear it to shreds?" I wondered. God wouldn't even allow me to cry. Doesn't a priest have the right to the attachment of at least one daughter?" And the answer was no! I was left with a feeling of total emptiness.

St. John of the Cross summarized the journey to the heart of the Father in two words, "toda...nada" which means everything...nothing. Its only when we have absolute nothing that we will have everything. But that won't happen without a major conversion experience. Only then will we reach the heart of God the Father. But that number will be extremely small.

Go back and read the story of Gideon (Judges 7). His army started with 32,000 men. God the Father told Gideon to tell those who were afraid or fearful to leave and go home. 22,000 left, 10,000 remained. That was too many, God the Father wanted the victory to belong to him. So he told Gideon that only those who drank water like dogs would be chosen. Just 300 men were allowed to take part in the battle, what a small remnant!

My prayer will always be that we are chosen to fight in the army of Mary to defeat Satan. Are we going to be part of the 300, to take part in the Triumph of the Immaculate Heart? Only those who reach the heart of the Father will be involved in this small remnant. The rest of us can only follow Padre Pio's injunction... "pray, hope and don't worry."

Chapter 13
The Triumph of the
Immaculate Heart of Mary
The Return to God the Father

"Just so, it is no part of your heavenly Father's plan that a single one of these little ones shall ever come to grief."
(Matthew 18:14)

"In this third year the sense of being on a 'journey to the Father' should encourage everyone to undertake, by holding fast to Christ the Redeemer of man, a journey of authentic conversion."[lxxiv]
*(Pope John Paul, II * Tertio Millennio Adventiente)*

"God who created man out of love also calls him to love – the fundamental and innate vocation of every human being. For man is created in the image and likeness of God who is himself love."[lxxv]
(Catechism of the Catholic Church)

"I have announced to you the Triumph of my Immaculate Heart in the world. In the end my Immaculate Heart will triumph."[lxxvi]
(Fr. Gobbi)

The Father's Will

As I prayed about the Father's will, I realized how intimately involved the Father has been in my life. In 1957 after I had been released from the seminary because of poor health, Archbishop Rummel told me: "son you won't live long enough to make it worthwhile ordaining you." As I sat on the St. Charles streetcar that day I recall speaking to the Father. "Father I thought I was one of your favorite sons. You sure have a strange way of treating your favorites." Yet I did return to the seminary and now after

40 years of the priesthood, I am the only survivor in New Orleans of the class of 1959. The rest died or quit the priesthood.

I decided to publish our parish jubilee retreat in the hopes that a few priests will use these beautiful testimonies and allow their parishioners the opportunity to experience the presence of God the Father through the Holy Spirit. The Holy Spirit put it all together for me thirteen years ago with the help of one of my deceased classmates, Fr. Emile LaFranz. I realized that our parish story would help those Catholics who left their faith because they didn't know you can be a born-again Catholic.

The Father had one of his daughters named Mary write to me from Morgan City, La. On June 29, 1999. She wrote, "I belong to a group of women who are very concerned with the falling away of so many Catholics from the Church. In our area five new churches have sprung up. Eighty percent of the congregation in these churches is made up of former Catholics. Some of the pastors of these churches are ex-Catholics. Something needs to be done if we are to stop the flood of Catholics leaving our holy church."

I plan to use the gift I received for my anniversary to publish and distribute a book called, *Finding God the Father*, as a gift to my parishioners. We need some tool to save the little ones that otherwise will be lost. "Just so, it is not part of your heavenly Father's plan that a single one of these little ones shall ever come to grief."(Matthew 18:14)

Restoring of God the Father's Kingdom on Earth

In teaching us the prayer, the "Our Father", Jesus laid out the plan that God has for us. Jesus said: "Thy kingdom come thy will be done, on earth as it is in heaven." (Matthew 10) It's the kingdom of God the Father that we are called upon to restore. It's the Father's will we must seek. Scripture tells us that the restoration of the kingdom on earth will be accomplished at a time designated by the Father (Acts 1:6)

Recently I read a book entitled *The Fatima Prophecies*, by Dr. Thomas Petrisko. I met Tom in Philadelphia a few years ago and have great respect for him and his work. There is much to be learned in this well researched work. Dr. Petrisko quotes Fr. Galot, a biblical scholar from the Pontifical Gregorian University in Rome. "... the answer to all our problems is to be found in God the Father:

> Learning to know God our Father is the supreme achievement of theology and, in a more all-embracing way, of all human knowledge. .... We must admit that until now scholarly effort to understand God our Father has not been as intense as it should have been. The most sublime object of all research and knowledge has not sufficiently challenged the minds of theologians. Our Christian faith has not adequately emphasized the person of God the Father, and liturgical worship has not focussed enough on this divine Person. Likewise, the kingdom whose coming is desired is the kingdom of the Father. It is, therefore, the reign of a fatherly love that gathers men into one sonship from which the closest brotherhood results. When Jesus said to 'seek his kingdom,' he was speaking to his disciples of the kingdom of 'your Father' (cf. Lk 12:30-31). The fatherhood of God gives a new meaning to the kingdom."[lxxvii]

The Fatherhood of God in Sacred Scripture

"Pope John Paul II explores this Fatherhood of God in Holy Scripture:

> "The mystery of the divine paternity within the Trinity was not yet explicitly revealed in the

194

Old Testament. However, the whole context of the Old Covenant was rich with allusians *to God's Fatherhood* in a moral and analogical sense. *Thus God is revealed as Father of his people,* Israel, when he commands Moses to ask for their liberation from Egypt: 'The Lord says Israel is my first-born son, and I say to you "Let my son go..." (Ex 4:22-23). ....

Jesus frequently announced, in the fullness of the Messianic times, God's fatherhood in regard to humanity by linking it with the numerous expressions contained in the Old Testament. Thus it expresses divine providence in regard to creatures, especially man: "Your heavenly Father feeds them...' (Mt 6:26; cf. Lk 12:24); 'Your heavenly Father knows that you need them all' (Mt 6:32; cf. Lk 12:30). Jesus sought to make the divine mercy understood by presenting as proper to God the welcoming reception of the Father for the prodigal son (cf. Luke 15:11-32). He exhorted those who heard his word 'be merciful, even as your Father is merciful' (Luke 6:36)."[lxxviii]

God the Father's Role in the Triumph of the Immaculate Heart of Mary

I believe that Our Blessed Mother has been leading, the Church, the faithful and the world to a reunion with God the Father. This is "...the final element of the Triumph of the Immaculate Heart of Mary, the crowning jewel of Mary's ... era of intercession, the presentation of God's children from the hands of their mother into the loving arms of God the Father."[lxxix]

Dr. Petrisko quotes: "Mary's message through interior locution to Father Gobbi at Fatima on May 7, 1997:

I (Mary) have caused to spring up here, for twenty-five years now, my Marian Movement of Priests so that the message of Fatima, often contested and rejected by many, might in your days come to its complete fulfillment.

Its fulfillment is necessary for you, my children, threatened and stricken, so that you may attain salvation. Its fulfillment is necessary for the Church, so wounded and crucified, so that from its painful and bloody trial, it might emerge all beautiful, without spot or wrinkle, in imitation of its heavenly Mother. Its fulfillment is necessary for all humanity, so that IT MAY RETURN TO THE ARMS OF ITS FATHER and come to know the new times of its full communion of love and of life with its Lord and God.

As of now, this plan of mine is being fulfilled with the Triumph of my Immaculate Heart in the world (MAY 8,1997)."[lxxx]

To put it very simply Our Blessed Mother is telling us that her triumph will come about when we all return to the arms of God the Father. The victory over Satan in which Mary is allowed to crush the head of Satan (Revel 12) is going to occur when all of her children are presented by her to God the Father. When every prodigal son and daughter returns to the Father that will be her TRIUMPH OF INTERCESSION.

Consecration and Feast Day to Father

In another message Mary gave to Father Gobbi, she said that the Triumph of the Immaculate Heart of Mary will take place by the year 2000. If this message is valid, there is very little time left. What does the Father want us to do? What is THE WILL OF THE FATHER FOR US?

We will seek, as a parish, to celebrate our love for GOD THE FATHER. We have ordered 1200 copies of a pamphlet entitled *Consecration and Feast Day for the*

Father of All Mankind. This is an eight day consecration to the eternal Father inspired by the Holy Spirit. It is my hope that Consecration to God Our Father will help our community develop a great love for God the Father.

On the first Sunday of August, we will honor God the Father in a special way. We will make the consecration to God the Father that he requested of Mother Eugenia. I had never heard of Mother Eugenia until I read the wonderful work by Tom Petrisko entitled *The Fatima Prophecies.* In this book Dr. Petrisko tells of an apparition on July 1, 1932 that Mother Eugenia received from the Eternal Father. In 1935, Bishop Alexander Caillot of Grenoble, France, convened a Commission of Inquiry. ... the commission took ten years ..."[lxxxi] but in 1945 the Bishop declared his opinion in favor of these apparitions. This decision has never been revoked.

It is not the purpose of this book to question whether the Church should have a special Feast Day and consecration to God our Father. We, priests and laymen alike, all know that PRIVATE REVELATIONS ARE NOT A MATTER OF CATHOLIC DOGMA. You can deny the apparitions at Fatima, Lourdes, Garabandal, etc and still be a Catholic in good standing.

I desire with all my heart to love the Father. It is my fondest hope that our entire community at St. Margaret Mary Church will fall in love with God the Father. I desire only to do his will. I believe it is the will of the Father that he be honored on a special day. We will honor God the Father on Sunday, August 1, 1999. We will honor the Father by publicly consecrating ourselves to him at Sunday Mass. I will also ask every parishioner to consider honoring the Father by distributing a FREE COPY of this book to all those who live in our parish.

Mother Eugenia received the following private revelation from God the Father:

"I desire to be known, loved, and honored with a special devotion. I do not ask for anything extraordinary. I desire only this: that one day or at least a Sunday, be dedicated to honoring Me in a special way under the title of Father of all Mankind. ... It is not difficult to find the texts in the Holy Scriptures. If you prefer to offer Me this special devotion on a Sunday, I choose the First Sunday of August."[lxxxii]

Consecration to God the Father

"The most compelling precedent for consecrating ourselves to God Our Father over an eight-day feast, or octave, is found in John 10:22-39."[lxxxiii] In the final three verses 36-39 Jesus says, "... do you claim that I blasphemed when, as he whom the Father consecrated and sent into the world, I said, 'I am God's Son'? If I do not perform me Father's works, put no fiath in me. But if I do perform them, even though you put no faith in me, put faith in these works, so as to realize what it means that the Father is in me and I in him."

In the passage above "... Jesus, during the eight-day Feast of Dedication, revealed that He was consecrated to God Our Father."[lxxxiv] The formula for Consecration can be found in the appendix.

The significance of consecrating ourselves on the first Sunday of August, "... is that it provides us with an opportunity (1) to honor God Our Father, (2) to offer Him our 'fiat,' and (3) to consecrate ourselves to Him. In this way, we are truly cooperating with our Mother Mary in the Triumph of Her Immaculate Heart. We are returning to our Father; we are offering Him our unconditional 'fiat' as Mary and Jesus did; and we are consecrating ourselves to Him – totally. As He so richly deserves, we are finally knowing, loving, serving, and honoring Him as God Our Father."[lxxxv]

Fatima Leads to the Father – The Final Vision

On June 13,1929 Sister Lucia, the remaining visionary from Fatima, experienced the "Last Vision" of Fatima in the Dorothean convent chapel in Tuy, Spain. It was a vision of the Holy Trinity made public only after Pope Paul VI's Fatima pilgrimage in 1967. Sister Lucia recently celebrated her 50 anniversary, May 31,1999 in a Carmelite convent. When I visited this May I was told by her nephew, Fr. Valinhos that Sister Lucia still has private apparitions of Our Lady. The picture on the front of this book is that "final vision of Fatima", received by Sister Lucia.

"In her own words Lucia describes the vision:
Suddenly the whole chapel was illuminated by a supernatural light, and a cross of light appeared above the altar, reaching to the ceiling. In a bright light at the upper part of the cross could be seen the face of a man and his body to the waist (Father) on his breast there was a dove also of light (Holy Spirit) and, nailed to the cross, was the body of another man (Son). Somewhat above the waist, I could see a chalice and a large host suspended in the air, on to which drops of blood were falling from the face of Jesus Crucified and from the wound in His side. These drops ran down on to the host and fell into the chalice. Our Lady was beneath the right arm of the cross (...it was Our Lady of Fatima with her Immaculate Heart ...in her left hand ... with a crown of thorns and flames...). Under the left arm of the cross, large letters, as of crystal clear water which ran down over the altar, formed these words: Graces and Mercy. [lxxxvi]*

The Meaning of the Final Vision

As I prayed about the meaning of the final vision of Fatima, that was made public in 1964, I could not help but wonder. What is Our Lady trying to tell us by making public a vision that was seen by Sister Lucia 35 years earlier? It is not simply a pretty picture meant to inspire us.

I believe that it could well hold the key not only to the **Triumph of the Immaculate Heart of Heart, but it could be an indication of the role of God the Father. The Father wants all of his children to come home!**

If you look carefully at the picture of the front of this book you notice a number of interesting things. What struck me about this vision is that it could hold out the answer to a prayer uttered by Jesus himself. Christ prayed: **"father that they may all be one as you are in me and I in you, that they all may be one in us."** It is clear from the encyclical of Pope John Paul II *Ut Unum Sint* that his greatest desire is the unification of the Church of Jesus Christ, that we may all be one.

I believe this picture holds the key. Our blessed Mother has told visionaries, i.e. at Garabandal and Medjugorje that a sign will be given, which will be a EUCHARISTIC MIRACLE. The Eucharistic miracle will follow a severe WARNING. If the world repents accepts the sign then an ERA OF PEACE WILL OCCUR. The vision of Sister Lucia, if it occurs publicly, would be a "eucharistic miracle"

A United Church

1. The Church would become One, if all Christians accepted the Eucharistic as the BODY AND BLOOD OF CHRIST. Obviously this would entail accepting the Mass as the "unbloody sacrifice of Calvary", and the priesthood. You notice in this picture that drops of blood are falling from Jesus into a chalice. A white host is Suspended above the chalice. Jesus death on the cross was a "bloody sacrifice". The mass in which the bread and wine are changed into the body and blood of

Christ is an "unbloody sacrifice", This vision of Sister Lucia is clearly Eucharistic. Holy Communion is truly Jesus.

2. The Church would be One, if all Christians accepted Mary, in her proper role as AN INTECESSOR. Catholics must clearly understand that as MEDIATRIX O GRACE, MARY'S INTERCESSION goes thorugh Her son, Jesus Christ. Mary's title of 'co-redemptrix, with Christ, does not mean "equal to" but a cooperater in the grace of redemption through her intercession.

A simple example will suffice those who are like little children. At Cana, it was Mary who noticed they had run out of wine. She did two things. She told her son, "they have no wine". In other words she brought it to his attention. ...that's intercession. Mary did a second thing, she told the wine stewards, "do whatever he tells you". Mary was a conduit, for the grace that Jesus brought about, the miracle of changing water into wine. In short she was a "necessary cooperator, as well as intercessor" in getting more wine. When Protestants accept the role of Mary as Intecessor, co-redeemer and advocate, the Church will be one. Co-redeemer is not "equal redeemer" but "redeemer with" Jesus Christ.

"We have been provided with a beautiful means to return to God Our Father, a progressive process that is described by St. Louis DeMontfort in *The Secret of Mary*: 'If the falsely enlightened, whom the devil has so miserably illusioned, even in prayer, had known how to find Mary, and through her to find Jesus, and through Jesus, God the Father, they would not have had such terrible falls. The saints tell us that when we have once found Mary, and through Mary, Jesus, and through Jesus God the Father, we have found all good. ... Our spiritual journey, then, is a dynamic process which takes us through Mary to Jesus in union with the Holy Spirit back **home to God Our Father.** This is the reason of our existence." [lxxxvii]

3. The Church will be one when Catholics begin to be open to the power of **the Holy Spirit**. The Holy Spirit is a conduit of grace from the Father through the Son. Born again Christians and Pentecostals have put Catholics to shame because so many of us, have refused to use the power of the Holy Spirit. I believe issue of healing in the church will be a clear indication to many in the future, that Roman Catholics have neglected the power of the Holy Spirit. The church will be One when all of God the Father's children are willing to be empowed by the Holy Spirit.

"At the end of the third session of the Second Vatican Council an Orthodox theologian Nikos Nissiotis, published an article in T*he Ecumenical Review* ... which said, in effect, that if the Council Documents did not say more about the Holy Spirit they would have little impart in the Orthodox Church.[lxxxviii]

As a result, "... there is much about the Holy Spirit in the conciliar texts which issued during the fourth session. Then Pope Paul VI publicly urged Catholic teachers and pastors to add to the theology of the Church and that of Our Lady that had come from the Council, a theology of the Holy Spirit. ... John Paul II has, in public discourses and writings, taught more on the Holy Spirit than all his predecessors together. He is the first Pope to declare a Year of the Holy Spirit."[lxxxix]

4. The Church will be One when Jesus is truly Lord of our lives. As important as accepting and proclaiming Jesus as Lord is, there is more that is needed. Jesus will be Lord in the church when we adore him truly present in Eucharistic adoration. Jesus will be Lord when we receive him in Holy Communion worthily. "He who eats my flesh and drinks my blood will have eternal life" (John 6). Jesus meant this literally. Otherwise when the crowd that had just witnessed a miracle of the multiplication of loves began to leave he would have

shouted... "come back." I didn't really mean this "literally...it was only meant figuratively. In fact, Christ allowed them to leave...because they did not have the faith to accept him at his word. Little children seven years old know, when I ask them...who is it you receive in Holy Communion? They respond immediately...it is Jesus. When everyone in the church can accept the "real presence of Jesus in the Eucharist", the church will be one.

You notice the nun kneeling under the images of God the Father, the Holy Spirit, Jesus and Mary. I believe that nun was St Margaret Mary. Hundreds of churches now have Perpetual Adoration as we have had for many years. This is a powerful example for our children, we really believe in the real presence of Jesus in the Eucharist.

5. Finally the Church will be One when we all take God the Father seriously. You have learned earlier in this book, that the 'Triumph of the Immaculate Heart", is simply Mary as intercessor, begging God the Father to bring his children home to him.

Mary is seen in pictures and statures around the world weeping. This is a simple way to teach children that their sins are driving them far from the Father's house. Mary wants all of her children, who are sinners and who is not, to return to the heart of God the Father.

The Church will be one, when the ecclesiatical leaders, the big brother in Rembrandt's painting, admits that all churches have sinned. When churches began to seek the will of God the Father and not their own will, the church will truly be one

In sister Lucia's vision God the Father plays an important role. He seems to be drawing us close to his heart. The Holy Spirit seems in the picture to be his heart.

God the Father wants him children to come home, all of his prodigal children.

Graces and Mercy

These two words, like crystal water in Sister Lucia's vision run down on the altar. It seem to me that this is a promise of God the Father, that He will FIND US, But the prodigal sons and daughters must recognize our SINFULNESS. The Church itself must acknowledge its sinfulness, in order to receive divine mercy the Church, as well as every member, must make this **journey home to the father. Then we truly will be one**.

Conclusion

It has been a long journey for me personally. For 40 years as a priest, I have, like so many of my brother priests, struggled. Many of them left the priesthood. Those of us who stayed were considered the misfits. Those who left were the heroes; we like St. Paul were considered the fools.

My journey to the Father took me to Medjugorje in 1987. I was seeking the Father's love but I left like a complete failure. In my own mind I was the "prodigal son." I had gone from a success working in the chancery in charge of building and insurance to becoming a pastor in Slidell. I was quickly told I would never fill the previous pastor's shoes. He had died at 52. Fr. Tim was well liked; I was shy and hesitant.

I also saw myself as the older brother in Rembrant's painting. I stayed in the priesthood, I didn't run away. I was restless and angry. The church held celibacy up as an ideal and I lived to see many of our best young men quit. In 1970 the synod of Rome was held on the priesthood. Celibacy was not discussed. I was jealous of those who quit the priesthood. I didn't have the courage, I thought, to leave. In truth Our Blessed Mother refused to let me go. Mary never gave up on me.

My journey to the Heart of the Father began as I wept in the room of apparition in Medjugorje. Mary was my intercessor before the Father. Satan has done everything in his power. She has placed St. Michael as my special protector, as she has done for every Marian priest in the world.

The Father did not reveal himself to me immediately. Learn one lesson at a time, seemed to be his modus operandi. I wrote a small book entitled *A Priest Looks at Medjugorje*. The Father wanted me to see myself as this little child on Mary's lap. I just wanted to say to her, "I love you." And Mary wanted to tell all of her priest sons, "I love you too!"

God the Father then sent Our Lady with two incredible crosses. In 1994 I was given a religious experience which was called "the illumination" at Garabandal. This mother of mine walked me through the need for a conversion experience. I saw my real sinfulness, my shame of my priesthood. I did just what I was told to do, to bring my children to penance and conversion. Twelve hundred adults signed up for confession on March 14, 1994. However, the Father felt I needed to learn to become a little child. So I ended up that night in a mental hospital. It was here I prayed, "Show me the Father!"

In 1995 I had to learn a little about suffering. I had an acute aortic aneurysm. Half those who have this surgery die, a number can never swallow again. I was left with a paralyzed vocal cord. It was after this I wrote a third book, *The Third Millennium: The Triumph of Our Lady*.

In June 1999 we had our adult retreat at St. Margaret Mary Church. We have a professional video of the retreat. We will sell the series of three tapes at cost $30.00 (to order: 504-643-6124) to any pastor who wishes to put on a "jubilee retreat." I knew from the experience of our high school students that a "Life in the Spirit" retreat would work. It was an amazing sight to see 600 adult Catholics proclaiming Jesus as Lord of their lives. For hours on Friday and Saturday night, Helen and Mike Rozeluk, our prayer team and myself prayed over adults for a born-again experience. Adult Catholics need to experience the Holy Spirit.

The End of the Story

I believe that my journey to the Father is nearly complete. God the Father has finally found me. **I did not find the Father.** The Father has given me a heart burning love for him. He has stripped me of everything others value, given me sufferings, and taken my most precious daughter, Kelly through suicide. However, God the Father has released me from my sense of shame. I now glory in being a priest of Jesus Christ. Regardless of what the world thinks of me, I know in loving Our Blessed Mother Mary, I am pleasing not only her son Jesus, who is the Lord of my life; I am pleasing God who is my loving Father.

Come Home to the Father

The message of this book is not only that Catholics can have a born again experience like Protestants. The Great Jubilee will usher in the Triumph of the Immaculate Heart of Mary. That means that God the Father's plan will soon be realized. All of his children will have an opportunity to return to the arms of God the Father, through the intercession of the Immaculate Heart of Mary. Jesus will then truly be the Lord of our lives. Then the desire of Jesus Christ will be heard ... that they all may be one.

John Bosco's Vision

The Father sent me a picture of St. John Bosco's vision. A pope is steering a ship in troubled waters. Two towers are protecting the ship. Mary is on one pillar, the Eucharist is on the other. From this image came the work, *The Remnant Church*. Only those parishes devoted to belief in the real presence of Jesus in the Eucharist and love of Mary, as well as support for the pope will be part of the remnant.

As we indicated earlier in the book, that the third millenium is a two edged sword. Pope John Paul II is looking for an outpouring of grace. Yet our Blessed Mother is warning us around the world of trials and tribulations. Mary has indicated that God the Father will give the world a spectacular warning. If we repent, following the Eucharistic warning, an era of peace will occur.

Certainly a comet might well be used as a predictable warning. It has been said that a comet appeared prior to the destruction of Jerusalem (70 A.D. Josephus). A comet appeared prior to World war I. On September 9,1999, according to Japanese astrologers, a comet will appear, though it may not be visible to the naked eye.

Day of Atonement

On the internet, I learned that Comet Lee was discovered by Japanese astronomers. It will be closest to the earth on September 9, 1999. The Jewish feast of Rosh Hashanah will be celebrated this year on September 10 & 11.

On the Feast of Atonement, **prior to the destruction of Jerusalem in 70 A.D.**, the entire Jewish nation was required to observe a strict fast. The High Priest, who had been "...kept awake during the whole preceding night and had taken a ritual bath in the morning, offered the morning sacrifice. Then he took off his high priest's dress, took a second bath, and vested himself with the simple white garment of a priest. In this attire, without the sign of his rank, he appeared as a sinner and conducted the ritual of atonement. ... The Israelites understood the significance of this feast, ...from the penitential character of this day, the repeated confession of sins by the high priest, and the various sprinkling with blood. Not only the sins of the priests and the people, committed during the entire year, had to be expiated, but even the sanctuary and the court had to be cleansed from all defilement. ... All of these rites must have taught the people the sanctity of God and His laws, as well as their own sinfulness and punishability."[xc]

If God the Father, who had a Jewish son, wanted to warn the world, what better way than a comet passing close to us on the Feast of the Atonement. Never forget the simple lesson I learned from God the Father. He will do anything he has to in order to bring his children to his heart. Jesus himself told us in Matthew's gospel, "God the Father desires that not one of his little ones be lost." The Father may have to scare them to death to get their attention.

By now dear reader, you realize that we do not find God the Father, he finds us. My prayer for each of you is this: May God the Father find you, as he found me. He found me hiding in the heart of Mary. This is not a time of fear or anxiety. It doesn't matter whether a comet comes or doesn't come. It is a time of great hope. God the Father will find you too, if you become like a little child. The Father will find you if you recognize that you are a sinner. If you willingly take up your cross daily Jesus will become the Lord of your life. If you ask the Holy Spirit, he will teach you the meaning of the final vision of Sr. Lucia. You will yearn to received the body and blood of Jesus Christ in the Eucharist, and worship the Son of God present under the appearance of simple bread. If you truly love Jesus you will honor and respect his mother Mary, and she in turn will say to the Father, "Heavenly Father I would like to present to you your son or daughter."

Do what I did and hide under the mantle of Mary; hang on to her apron strings. That is how I found myself, hiding in her heart, when through her intercession, **God the Father found me.** What joy there will be in heaven, when the Heavenly Father says to each of us. "You are my beloved son ... You are my beloved daughter, on you my favor rests!"

That is the plan of God the Father!

A Very Special Prayer to God Our Father

"At the core of the revelations to Mother Eugenia Ravasio is a very special prayer reportedly given to her by the Eternal Father called God is My Father. It reads:

My Father in Heaven, how sweet it is to know that You are my Father and that I am your child!

Especially when the skies of my soul are cloudy and my cross weighs more heavily, I feel the need to repeat to You: Father, I believe in Your love for me!

Yes, I believe that You are a Father to me at every moment of my life, and that I am Your Child!

I believe that You love me with an infinite love!

I believe that You are watching over me night and day and that not a hair falls from my head without Your permission!

I believe that, in Your infinite Wisdom, You know better than I what is good for me.

I believe that, in Your infinite power, You can bring good even out of evil.

I believe that, in Your infinite goodness, You make everything to the advantage of those who love You; even under the hand of those who strike me, I kiss Your hand which heals!

I believe, but increase in me faith, hope, and love!

Teach me always to see Your love as my guide in every event of my life.

Teach me to surrender myself to You like a baby in its mother's arms.

Father, You know everything, You see everything, you know me better than I know myself; You can do everything, and You love me!

My Father, since it is Your wish that we should always turn to You. I come with confidence to ask You, together with Jesus and Mary... (Request the favor you desire.)

For this intention, and uniting myself to their Most Sacred Hearts, I offer You all my prayers, my sacrifices and mortifications, all my actions, and greater faithfulness to my duties (*).

Give me the light, the grace, and the power of the Holy Spirit!

Strengthen me in this Spirit, that I may never lose Him, never sadden Him, and never allow Him to become weaker in me.

My Father, I ask this in the name of Jesus, Your Son! And you, Jesus, open Your Heart and place in it my own, and, together with Mary's offer it to our Divine Father! Obtain for me the grace that I need!

Divine Father, call all men to Yourself. Let all the world proclaim Your Fatherly Goodness and Your Divine Mercy!

Be a tender Father to me and protect me wherever I am, like the apple of Your eye. Make me always a worth son/daugher; have mercy on me!

Divine Father, sweet hope of our souls, may You be known, honored, and loved by all men!

Divine Father, infinite goodness poured out on all peoples, may You be known, honored, and loved by all men!

Divine Father, beneficent dew of humanity, may You be known, honored, and loved by all men!

(*)If this prayer is to be recited as a novena, add: 'I promise to be more generous, especially during these nine days, in a given circumstance, to such and such a person...'"

Partial indulgence
Jean, Cardinal Verdier
Archbishop of Paris,
May 8, 1936

Appendix

"The primary tasks of the preparation for the Jubilee thus include a renewed appreciation of the presence and activity of the Spirit, who acts within the Church both in the Sacraments, ... and in the variety of charisms, roles and ministries which he inspires for the good of the Church."
(Pope John Paul, II)

"There are sacramental graces, gifts proper to the different sacrament. There are furthermore special graces, also called charisms after the Greek term used by St. Paul and meaning 'favor,' 'gratuitous gift,' 'benefit.' Whatever their character - sometimes it is extraordinary, such as the gift of miracles or of the tongues ... are intended for the common good of the Church. They are at the service of charity which builds up the Church."
(Catechism of the Catholic Church)

The Gift of Inner Healing

At a priest's retreat at San Giovanni Rotondo, the monastery in which the late Padre Pio lived, Ms. Kathleen Keefe had gathered a group of priests for a Divine Mercy Retreat, July 1994. The retreat was entitled "Heal the Shepherd, Heal the Flock." The retreat master was Fr. Bernard J. Bush, S.J. Ph.D. It was an extraordinary opportunity for me personally to begin a process of inner healing.

At this retreat I had the opportunity of meeting Fr. Al Fredette. Fr. Fredette has been a pioneer in prayers for inner healing as well as ancestral healing. He was a great blessing to the priests who attended the retreat in San Giovanni. He was able to minister to us and was quite generous in sharing the material he has accumulated over the years.

There is a new book entitled *The Power Among us*, the story of a healing ministry. It was complied and edited by Patricia Kelly Ph.D. Dr. Kelly compiled a complete program of inner healing, which has compromised much of the work of Fr. Al Fredette. It has an explanation of inner healing as well as healing of the family tree. It also provides in one location all of the prayers needed by the priest for a "Mass of Inner Healing". It can be purchased from Queenship Publishing Company. Fr. Fredette may be reached by writing to:

Fr. Fredette
La Salette
947 Park Street
Attleboror, MA. 02703
Telephone: (508) 222-5410

Fr. Fredette gave the priests at the retreat a copy of the genogram together with a page of the appropriate symbols. There are thousands of possible defects in our own family tree. See genogram and explanation at the end of the book.

Sacred Scripture speaks of the sins of parents being visited on their children down to the third and fourth generation. Fr. Fredette lists some general characteristics to look for.

1) Inherited spiritual defects: from prayerlessness to atheism.
2) Inherited physical defects: such as cancer & heart conditions.
3) Inherited emotional defects: from shyness to tendencies to suicide.
4) Inherited psycho-social defects: from poor spouse communication to unemployment and crime.
5) Inherited social defects: such as divorce, child abuse, etc.

As a religion teacher many years ago I was called by one of my students. Her father had bodily thrown her out of her house. I picked the young woman up and returned to her home, convincing her father he had acted impulsively. He agreed to take his daughter back.

A week later we were discussing in class, "problem children." "If my kids give me any trouble I will just hit them," the same young woman responded without thinking. Because her father had abused her, she was preparing herself to use abuse when she became a mother.

Healing Prayer of Ancestry

Fr. Al Fredette has graciously given his permission to reproduce information on Inner Healing. I would urge Pastors to consider offering a Mass of Inner Healing to help your parishioners deal with shame in their lives.

NOTE: The following three prayers (Healing of Ancestry, Deliverance Prayer, and A Healing Prayer for Family Healings) are recited after communion during the Mass of Inner Healing.

Healing of Ancestry

Eternal Father,

As a community of faith and a family in prayer, we gather to give you praise, adoration and thanksgiving in all things. We pray for all the deceased members of the families represented here, and all those who, in the past, were born deceased still born, miscarried, aborted, never committed to God and those who died an early death. We pray for the family members who died brutally or violently, lost in the war or otherwise died from strange and mysterious illnesses, from great fears, acts of cowardice, sudden death, in mysterious fires and for all who were rejected by the family, wanderers and lost members, adopted, abandoned, or rejected.

We pray for all the members of the families represented here who were addicted to drugs, alcohol, games, compulsions of all kinds, gambling, lust, deceitfulness, addictive shopping, and for all family members unduly attached to values of the world, money, prestige, power and control over persons or things.

We pray for those who died and were never prayed for and those buried without a proper funeral. We pray for those who died by their own hand and for those who were murderers or accomplices. We pray for those who died through suffocation or were abandoned, for those afflicted with great phobias, emotional instability; insanity, unexplained illness and from all other causes known by God alone.

We ask release from all bondage coming from the occult, under any form practiced by family members in the past or in the present affecting living members in whatever negative form of bondage, illness, infirmity, emotional or physical illnesses, addictions of any kind, spiritual torment or otherwise confused. I hereby rebuke and cast out in the Name of Jesus Christ, from all living members of these families, the following dark and binding forces of spiritual and emotional torment, undue anxieties, tensions and stress, violence, prejudice, error, devaluation, self-hatred, retaliation, arrogance and deceitful pride in all its forms.

We ask deliverance from fears of all kinds -- the fear of being found out, fear of commitment, fear of failure, the fear of ghosts, the fears of natural elements such as heights, thunder, lightning, wind, water, fire, closed spaces, fearful dreams, the fear of rejection, the fear of man, the fear of woman, the fear of darkness and all other kinds of fears, spiritual, emotional or physical from whatever source.

I hereby rebuke and cast out, in the Name of Jesus Christ all dark and binding forces of superstition, slander, destructive lies and falsehoods, deception in all its forms and attempts to destroy others' reputation, lust, homosexuality, lesbianism, incest and perversions of all kinds, obsessive and compulsive destructive behavior, manic attitudes, depressions, denial and deceitful games, abandonment, excessive anger and rage, guilt, vengeance and self-destructive anxieties, attitudes and attempts.

I hereby rebuke and cast out, in the Name if Jesus Christ, the following dark and binding forces called confusion, chaos, rebellion, arrogance, hallucinations, sleep walking, addictions, fortune telling in all its forms, witchcraft, Satanism, necromancy, santeria, black Mass, and occultism in all its forms.

In the Name of Jesus Christ, I rebuke and cast out all deceitful and destructive forces of despair, betrayal, uncontrolled frustrations, bitterness, despondency, repression, projection in all its forms, manipulation and control, the fear of rejection, self-deceit, rejection and self-rejection, exaggerated anxieties, withdrawal, self-pity, false guilt, masturbation and perversions of all kinds. I rebuke and cast out in the Name of Jesus Christ, the dark and binding forces of pride, denial, fantasies, doubt, mockery, repression, hopelessness, fear of insanity, fear of perdition, infidelity, abuse of all kinds, verbal, mental, emotional, physical, or spiritual, false gods and idols.

Seal, I break you in the Name of Jesus Christ.
(repeat the above line three times before continuing)

I hereby break and cast out in the Name of Jesus Christ curses of any kind placed upon the members of the families represented here and all ancestry of these families.

I hereby break and sever by the power of the Word of God and the Sword of the Spirit all negative ancestral spirits and influences of any kind from whatever source, genetic, spiritual, physical, emotional or psychic, affecting the living members of these families wherever they may now be living.

In the name of all these past and lost or injured souls, I ask forgiveness for those who died unforgiven and unforgiving. For them, we ask deliverance from present darkness, confusion and chaos. As a family, we raise up to God all the ancestors who were never baptized for whatever reason. We ask the Lord to accept them, through the baptism of desire, into the family of the Church with a right to Heaven. We bestow upon them all the names of family members who surrounded them at the time of their death. We command the Holy angels to lead all these souls into Paradise to be forever in the Presence of our heavenly Father, the angels, and the saints and from this moment on, to be intercessors for all the living members of the families represented here today. We claim the most Precious Blood of Jesus Christ upon all members of these families, that they be protected from all harm, injury, accident, illness and the wiles of the devil. We also ask the Holy Angels to be, now and always, sentries of protection for all the members of the families represented here today and we ask the angels to protect their possessions from all harm and destructive forces.

We make our prayers in the Name of Jesus of Nazareth whose compassionate love heals all wounds through forgiveness, mercy and prayer. AMEN

NOTE: After the first Healing of Ancestry Mass has been said ... it is important that you attend a Mass in your parish. After the Mass, pray this deliverance prayer so that there will be a continued healing of the living members of your family.

Deliverance Prayer

Dear Heavenly Father,
We praise and glorify you for your love and mercy that you have bestowed upon us and for the spirit of revelation working within us to reveal all hidden sins -- both our own and those from former generations. We now take authority in the name of Jesus Christ over all familial spirits, all generational bondage, all hereditary defects, genetic or of blood, or wrong inclinations that may have been transmitted to us from within our family tree or within spiritual families to which we belong, including the defects within the church that have had their effects upon us personally. By the faith that you give us, we rebuke all sin and the forces of evil that lead to sin. In the holy name of your son, Jesus Christ, we take authority over all familial spirits and bondage, and their manifestations within our lives. By that same power of Jesus, we break the power of evil from ourselves and our families and destroy what otherwise might by transmitted to our descendants. Help us to accomplish your perfect will and fill our hearts and minds with praise of you as we acknowledge your tender mercy. Thank you, Lord, for total healing and deliverance, in Jesus' precious name. AMEN.

A Healing Prayer for Family Healing

Father, I adore you and give you thanks for creating me to be just who I am, my genes, my life conditions, my space in life and time.

You created me to enjoy the fullness of life -- your life in me. I believe that you desire to make my family whole and that you have already begun to heal us in all the ways we need healing. Take away my built-in defenses this weekend. Remove all the barriers that prevent healing and my accepting fully your love for me and my family members. I look forward to the time in which your work will be completed and I believe that I will be a channel of that healing for my entire family.

Jesus, I ask for the grace I need to forgive all who have ever hurt me, and I ask to be a representative of my family in receiving grace for all who have hurt any members of my family, individually or collectively. I ask forgiveness from all whom we have hurt. Heal us of all experiences that have made us feel guilty and ashamed; that have caused us to be self-rejecting, and rejecting of one another. Heal me of the rejection real or imagined, of others. Heal me of ridicule and of any incidences in my life or in the life of my family members, that have made us feel unworthy or inferior.

(Take time for the Holy Spirit to bring incidents to your mind.)

Surround me with your light, Jesus, and penetrate the very depths of my being with that light. Let there remain no areas of darkness in me or in my family members, but transform our whole being with the healing light of your love. Open me completely to receive your love, Jesus. Thank you for being our family healer, and my personal healer. AMEN

✟✟✟✟

The Eucharist is a powerful means of healing the family tree. We are dealing not just with grace but with the author of grace, Jesus Christ, the Lord himself. Many scriptural passages in the Eucharistic celebration refer directly to the healing power including the ultimate healing "He who feeds on my flesh and drinks my blood has eternal life, and I will raise him up on the last day" (John 6:54.)[xci]

****

Genogram
Exodus 20:1-17

A reading from the Book of Exodus
The Law was given through Moses (John 1:17)

For I, the Lord, your God, am a jealous God, inflicting punishment for
their fathers' wickedness on the children of those who hate me, down to
the third and fourth generation: but bestowing mercy down to the
thousandth generation, on the children of those who love me and keep
my commandments.

All of us inherit both good and bad genes from our ancestors. It is
important that we be healed of all megative influences from the past up
to the third and fourth generation and all generations before these
where healing has not occurred.

This is what the Healing of Ancestry Mass and Deliverance Prayer
are all about. We forgive all of our ancestors who brought upon us and
our families negative influences. But, we need to rejoice and truly be
grateful to all who preceded us and transmitted to us the graces,
blessings and gifts we enjoy in our lives. These blessings flow on
generation to generation "down to the thousandth..." Today, we are
within that thousandth generation!

The Healing of Ancestry is sometimes referred to as an
Intergenerational Healing or Healing of the Family Tree.

Whenever we have a healing of ancestry Mass, it is like peeling an
onion. The first Mass and Deliverance Prayers seem to reach out to the
ancestors up to the third and fourth generation who preceded the
present generation. Bondages which existed in those now deceased are
released and all who had died without baptism for whatever reason
have now been lifted up in the baptism of desire, given a name and led
into Paradise by the angels where they belong with God, the angels and
saints and, as such, have become intercessors for all the living members
of your family. Healing is now occurring within the living as bondages
of ill-health, unforgiveness and all kinds of hurt and suffering begin to
be loosed as health and peace is restored to the family.

However, when the first layer of the onion is peeled and resolved,
a new layer appears exposing the problems and bondages of the living
members of the family. This oftentimes, requires a second Ancestry
Mass and a continued praying of the deliverance Prayer by family
members.

Question marks can be used for unknown persons, forgotten names, even possible ancestors of whose existence you may not be sure.

Since this is a prayer-focusing tool, and not a scientific genealogy, its completeness is not particularly relevant. God knows the individuals in the family tree, especially those who may need our prayerful help for release from bondage.

Other details are helpful to supply: ages at present, or a time of death. Color codes may be used for various personality characteristics or publicly known disorders: addictions, occult involvement (fortune telling, horoscopes, witchcraft), invalid marriages, diseases, mental illnesses, abnormalities.

Include also things like miscarriages, abortions, violent deaths, burial without Christian rites.

Remember that the genogram is meant only to help you specify your prayer intentions – thus also helping to intensify your faith. It can provide a visual framework for you to call the blood of Jesus upon individuals, living or dead, to help them, and to be applied, as it were, between each generation to block the transmission of sins' effects. It can also help to recognize situations in which there are repeated behavioral patterns or disorders.

Defects to Look for in the Family Tree

Potentially there are thousands of possible defects one can look for but usually they fall under several generic categories.

1) Inherited Spiritual Defects: from prayerlessness to atheism; including patterns of sin in your life, a besetting weakness, etc.
2) Inherited Physical Defects: from dandruff to diabetes; including cancer, heart problems, arthritis, etc.
3) Inherited emotional defects: from shyness to tendencies to suicide; including various neuroses, psychoses (be cautious about calling a psychological illness an inherited or generational illness if it is not!)
4) Inherited Psycho-Social Defects: from poor inter-spouse communication to psychopathic murder; including poverty, unemployment, crime, etc.
5) Inherited Social Defects: (common to entire families, nations, or ethnic groups) from in-law aloofness to mafia families; including divorce, machoism, child abuse, parent abuse, etc.

6) Strengths and Weaknesses of you and your ancestors back to the third and fourth generations (maternal and paternal lines): emotional states, physical states, spiritual conditions, athletic prowess, financial abilities, academic/intellectual abilities, behavioral patterns, habits, temperaments, besetting sins, involvement with false gods.

Genogram

---

[i] Nouwen, Henri, *The Return of the Prodigal Son: A Story of Homecoming,* (New York, N.Y., Doubleday, 1992), page 20.

[ii] IBID, pages 20-21.

[iii] IBID, page 22.

[iv] IBID, page 43.

[v] IBID, page 43.

[vi] IBID, page 76.

[vii] Pope John Paul, II, *Tertio Millennio Adventiente,* (Boston, Ma.: Pauline Books & Media, 1994.), page 53, #49.

[viii] *Catechism of the Catholic Church,* (New York: Catholic Book Publishing Co., 1992), page 377, #1508.

[ix] Pope John Paul, II, *Tertio Millennio Adventiente,* (Boston, Ma.: Pauline Books & Media, 1994.), page 38, #33.

[x] *Catechism of the Catholic Church,* (New York: Catholic Book Publishing Co., 1992), page 446-447, #1816.

[xi] Pope John Paul, II, *Tertio Millennio Adventiente,* (Boston, Ma.: Pauline Books & Media, 1994.), page 47, #40.

[xii] *Catechism of the Catholic Church,* (New York: Catholic Book Publishing Co., 1992), page 347, #1376.

[xiii] IBID, page 347, #1377.

[xiv] Bright, Bill, *Have You Heave of the Four Spiritual Laws,* (Orlando, Fl., New Life Publications, 1994.), page 2.

[xv] IBID, page 4.

[xvi] IBID, page 6.

[xvii] IBID, page 8.

[xviii] IBID, page 8 & 9.

[xix] IBID, page 9.

[xx] IBID, page 10.

[xxi] *Catechism of the Catholic Church,* (New York: Catholic Book Publishing Co., 1992), page 80, #305.

[xxii] Pope John Paul, II, *Tertio Millennio Adventiente,* (Boston, Ma.: Pauline Books & Media, 1994.), page 47, #40.

[xxiii] *Catechism of the Catholic Church,* (New York: Catholic Book Publishing Co., 1992), page 180, #685 & 686.

[xxiv] Pope John Paul, II, *Tertio Millennio Adventiente,* (Boston, Ma.: Pauline Books & Media, 1994.), page 59, #56.

[xxv] Martin, Ralph, *New Covenant Magazine,* pages 10-11, June 1999.

[xxvi] IBID

[xxvii] IBID

[xxviii] Martin, Ralph, *New Covenant Magazine,* pages 10-11, June 1999.

[xxix] IBID

[xxx] IBID

[xxxi] IBID

[xxxii] IBID

[xxxiii] IBID

[xxxiv] IBID

[xxxv] IBID

[xxxvi] IBID

[xxxvii] IBID

[xxxviii] IBID

[xxxix] IBID

[xl] *Catechism of the Catholic Church,* (New York: Catholic Book Publishing Co., 1992), page 337, #1336.

[xli] Pope John Paul, II, *Tertio Millennio Adventiente,* (Boston, Ma.: Pauline Books & Media, 1994.), page 57, #55.

[xlii] *Catechism of the Catholic Church,* (New York: Catholic Book Publishing Co., 1992), page 356, #1418.

[xliii] *IBID,* page 427, #1718.

[xliv] *IBID,* page 426-427, #1716.

[xlv] Pope John Paul, II, *Tertio Millennio Adventiente,* (Boston, Ma.: Pauline Books & Media, 1994.), page 43, #37.

[xlvi] *Catechism of the Catholic Church,* (New York: Catholic Book Publishing Co., 1992).

[xlvii] Pope John Paul, II, *Tertio Millennio Adventiente,* (Boston, Ma.: Pauline Books & Media, 1994.), page 50, #44.

[xlviii] St. Augustine, translated by Edward B. Pusley, D.D., *The Confession of Saint Augustine,* (New York, Random House, 1949), page 3.

[xlix] http://www.ourlady.ca/

[l] http://www.ourlady.ca/

[li] *Catechism of the Catholic Church,* (New York: Catholic Book Publishing Co., 1992), page 252, #969.

[lii] Pope John Paul, II, *Tertio Millennio Adventiente,* (Boston, Ma.: Pauline Books & Media, 1994.), page 56, #54.

[liii] *Catechism of the Catholic Church,* (New York: Catholic Book Publishing Co., 1992), page 391, #1563.

[liv] IBID, page 391, #1564.

[lv] IBID, page 391, #1566.

[lvi] Kawalski, Sister M. Faustina, *Divine Mercy in My Soul, Diary,* (Maria Press: Stockbridge, Massachusetts, 1987), pages 563-564, #1588.

[lvii] Breault, Fr. Joseph, *Seeking purity of Heart: The Gift of Ourselves to God,* (Living Flame Press: New York, 1975.)

[lviii] IBID, page 68.

[lix] IBID, page 70.

[lx] IBID, page 71.

[lxi] IBID, page 79-81.

[lxii] IBID, page 83.

[lxiii] IBID, page 84.

[lxiv] IBID, page 85.

[lxv] IBID, page 85.

[lxvi] IBID, page 85-86.

[lxvii] IBID, page 86.

[lxviii] IBID, page 86.

[lxix] IBID, page 89.

[lxx] IBID, page 90.

[lxxi] IBID, page 91.

[lxxii] *Catechism of the Catholic Church,* (New York: Catholic Book Publishing Co., 1992), page 676, #2818.

[lxxiii] Pope John Paul, II, *Tertio Millennio Adventiente,* (Boston, Ma.: Pauline Books & Media, 1994.), page 47, #40.

[lxxiv] IBID, page 54, #50.

[lxxv] *Catechism of the Catholic Church,* (New York: Catholic Book Publishing Co., 1992), page 401, #1604.

[lxxvi] Fr. Gobbi, Dec. 31, 1997.

[lxxvii] Petrisko, Thomas, *The Fatima Prophecies*, (St. Andrews Productions: McKees Rocks, Pa, 1998), page351-352 .

[lxxviii] IBID, pages 355-357.

[lxxix] IBID, pages 365-366

[lxxx] IBID, page 366

[lxxxi] IBID, page 363.

[lxxxii] IBID, page 363.

[lxxxiii] *God Our Father: Consecration and Feast Day for The Father of All Mankind,* (Pittsburgh, Pa., The Father of All Mankind Apostolate, 1998), page 3.

[lxxxiv] IBID, page 3.

[lxxxv] IBID, page 3.

[lxxxvi] Holy Card, Printed with ecclesiastical permission. Rev. Msgr. John B. Szymanski, Vicar General. Diocese of Metuchen, April 2, 1996. The Blue Arm of Our Lady of Fatima, Washington, NJ 07882.

[lxxxvii] *God Our Father: Consecration and Feast Day for The Father of All Mankind,* (Pittsburgh, Pa., The Father of All Mankind Apostolate, 1998), page 1.

[lxxxviii] IBID, page v.

[lxxxix] IBID, page v.

[xc] Steinmueller, S.T.D., John E., *A Companion to Scripture Studies,* (Joseph F. Wagner, Inc., New York City, N.Y., 1950), pages 346-348.

[xci] Carroll, Rev. Richard L., *The Third Millenium: The Triumph of Our Lady,* (Chelsea, Michigan, Book Crafters, 1996), pages 41 – 49.

*** All Bible Quotes, not already part of a direct quote, come from *The New American Bible*, (New York: Thomas Nelson Publishers, 1983).

*** The picture of St. Lucia's Final Fatima Vision on the front cover of this book is used with permission from Quadriga Art, Inc. 30 East 33rd Street, New York, NY 10016 © Reproducta Co., Inc.

*** The picture of Rembrandt's *Return of the Prodigal Son* on the back cover of this book is used with permission from Scala/Art Resource, 65 Bleecker St. (9th Floor) New York, NY 10012. Rembrandt Harmensz. Van Rijn. Return of the Prodigal Son, 1668-1669. Oil on canvas, 265x205 cm. Hermitage St. Petersburg, Russia.

Consecration Prayer of the Holy Octave of Consecration to God the Father

My Dearest Father, please accept this offering of myself – my body, mind, and soul:

I praise You for Your Creation – all Your works and wonders.

I thanks You for giving me life and for all that You have done for me.

I offer up to You all that You have so generously given me.

I am sincerely **sorry** for not knowing, loving, serving, and honoring You as I should.

I embrace my **inheritance** as Your child, both the joy and the responsibilities.

I give you my **"yes"** so that I may be an instrument of Your Will.

I pledge my **fidelity** and I ask for the grace of steadfastness and perseverance in my Faith.

Most loving, caring, and merciful of Father, in Your Divine Presence, I sincerely proclaim my love for You; I give myself (and my family) to You; and I solemnly **consecrate** myself (and my family) to You – now and forever.

Dearest Father, as Your child, I ask –

That You send Mary to guide me to Jesus, and that Jesus sends me the Holy Spirit so that they may all bring me to You.

That You dwell with me and in me – a living temple prepared by Mary, dedicated by Jesus, and purified by Your Holy Spirit. And may I always be with You and in You.

That You permit me, as Your child, to be Your true and intimate friend – one who loves You above all things.

And that you come for me when I die, to bring me home to You.

I further ask You, Father, for the sake of all mankind:

To have mercy on all Your children – past, present, and future.

To bring peace to the world and to gather all Your children to Yourself.

And that Your kingdom comes and Your Will is done on earth as it is in heaven.

Amen.[i]

---

[i] *God Our Father: Consecration and Feast Day for The Father of All Mankind,* (Pittsburgh, Pa., The Father of All Mankind Apostolate, 1998), page 32.